Early readers respond:

"An elegy of the highest order. The narrator's love and grief recall the most ancient myths while also subverting them. Her canine companion Gilgamesh becomes Enkidu, and she, Enkidu, becomes Gilgamesh. They merge into one being. Orpheus is now a witch whose song resonates across humanity, yet she mourns for the inhuman. She has the faith and wits to wait this time until she reemerges above ground before turning around to face death. Her beloved's tapetum eyes, his breath in her palm, the wilderness he senses with keen joy, the pain of her world without him, Rilke's panther, are all reborn in her exquisite words, a dog's tracks, stepping across these pages."
— Rebecca Snow, author of Glassmusic

"Again and again, darkness veils their eyes/and the palm of my left hand holds/the beloved's last breath, a burning city:

In Gilgamesh Wilderness, Jessamyn Smyth invokes a modern epic for readers to witness the earthen, luminous, yet also brittle remains of one soul being shared by two bodies; 'the infinite beloved' and the one who has been left behind.

Smyth's diction spindles from her fingers like an incantation while also anchoring the reader into the corporeal and incarnate stuff of earth. The owls, the wolves, the heft of ice crackling in a stream swollen with winter, and mostly, the embodiment (and disembodiment) of her beloved as they gallop and pinion and stalk and look up and bear witness to the birds in the trees (the way she speaks to her beloved!) as her language reflects their physical cadence together, the movement of both their union and even their being torn asunder.

Further, Smyth's frequent use of white space on the page speaks as elemental as the text - which often feels like white gulps of air, gulfs of absence and then the profound invisible presence within that dizzy blurred spot in an otherwise normal field of vision; *His face my scotoma,/the only constellation.*

Gilgamesh Wilderness delightfully and heartbreakingly breaks beyond the formal constraints of prose and poetry and reads like an inconsolable and jubilant poetic form of its own. It is a form that reminds me of Ann Carson's *Autobiography of Red* (and I hooted with pleasure when Smyth refers to it later in the text) in both its inventive leaps and kinship with mythic allusions to ages past, yet here in *Gilgamesh Wilderness*, I can feel more of what's at stake for the writer, and I can almost almost feel the alchemy of resurrection; the beat of the book's pulse in my hands, its breath, its head no longer lolling but very much alive.

When I felt the end of the book approaching, I wanted so very much to slow down. I wanted the book to stay, stay in my veins. I knew I would be bereft after I turned the final page, which is likely the pulse sensation of what Smyth was conjuring for her readers in the first place; to be invited to stay inside her skin, to become one soul shared between two bodies and to shush ourselves in order to Come further in. Further up. Listen.

Ultimately Smyth, like Gilgamesh before her, cannot kill death for us or for her infinite beloved, but if we listen close enough, we may hear the salve approximating an answer to that epic question:

how do we go on— heart open—
in the presence of death?
    How stupid and ineffectual, love that can't stop death.
    How valiant   and beautiful."
— Jim Churchill-Dicks, author of *Wine-Dark Mother and*
    the Trapper's Son

"...The rib-spreader open truth of *Gilgamesh Wilderness*. Like I'm reading Smyth say: 'Listen, the worst has already happened. You already love. You can stop holding against it. Put your heart into my hands, into my voice. Trust me and we will look together....'

There is only one story, as ancient as it is personal: how to carry a living heart through the glow of this burning world. Through

the gates of *Gilgamesh Wilderness*'s pages a singular voice is waiting for you. Luminous."
— Claudia Mauro, author of *Stealing Fire,*
    publisher at Whit Press

"Jessamyn Smyth's *Gilgamesh Wilderness* lives up to its mythic name by leading us on an arresting and dazzling journey. Smyth deftly intertwines stunning prose and poetry, narration and reflection, dreams and waking life. Reading this book reminds me of contemplating a beaver lodge. On the surface, it may appear accidental or collaged, with fragments and poems and stories arranged to seem almost random. But look deeply into a beaver lodge and you'll find arrangement, engineering, order. This book constructs a similar intentional complexity. Smyth might pull us through subterranean levels of unsparing grief and even submerge us in suffocating darkness, an immersion taking us to the edge of death itself. But she eventually leads us to a surface where the air is full of light and sound and life and even a sense of playful contentment as delightful as a wide tail slapping water. This line is going to stay with me for a while: 'that pulsing you see in the inside of her wrist, it's misleading…' The whole journey of this book is worth every step."
— John Sheirer, Author of *Stumbling Through Adulthood:*
    Linked Stories

"I love this book. Its words take me into my own head and heart and past — all my beloved dogs and woods and snowy bleak winters. I want my students to read it and see how to bring the old stories into their new ones and weave them together into something true and magical that will heal them, and walk with them as they grow. "
— Nora Streed, Director, Writing Center and ESL Services
    UNC School of the Arts

"In a wilderness of bone-deep grief, Jessamyn Smyth builds a word road as she travels. Lighting her way, mysteries as temporal and immediate as a single surprising bloom

opening to a full meadow of color and as close to eternal as the distant beckoning Milky Way. A paean to her companion and to deep love transcending species, *Gilgamesh Wilderness* gathers together startling poems, prose, and fragments of contemplation. Mixing the mythic and the muddy, Smyth's words invite us to walk with her and her familiar through a geography of the heart, from the Salish Sea to the Green Mountains and the Connecticut River Valley. From wondering how one can go on to going on. This is a stunning collection, polished with elegant, feral energy and insight."
— Jan Maher, author of *Heaven, Indiana* and *Earth As It Is*

"As I read deeper into *Gilgamesh Wilderness*, I think of all the people who need me to give them a copy…so many people will be moved by this book…"
— Elizabeth Macduffie, publisher of *Meat For Tea*

"*Gilgamesh Wilderness* is a keening. Part elegy, part eulogy, it is a brilliantly written lamentation about the loss of the beloved. That the beloved is a dog made these verses resonate all the more for me. Because this dog, like the warrior companion whose death sent the classical Gilgamesh into a spiral of grief, like the service dog whose ghost spirit still lives with me, is no doting lover, but an ally, a familiar, a friend. I struggle to put this into words, because I know (oh, do I know!) that this is not a "woman and dog" story. …I waited for this book, and it was worth the wait. Walk in the wilderness…and remember how fierce love can be."
— Michel Wing, author of *Body on the Wall*

Gilgamesh Wilderness

Gilgamesh Wilderness

Jessamyn Smyth

Saddle Road Press

Gilgamesh Wilderness © 2021 Jessamyn Smyth

Saddle Road Press
Ithaca, New York
saddleroadpress.com

All rights reserved. No part of this book may be reproduced or transmitted in any form or by any means without written permission of the author.

Cover photograph and book design by Don Mitchell
Author photograph by Rebecca Aldous

ISBN 9781736525838
Library of Congress Control Number: 2021940226

Books by Jessamyn Smyth

Koan Garden
Kitsune
The Inugami Mochi
Skaha

v1.1

What we have to do now is impossible.

It's all Dylan Thomas from here.

Contents

Unfamiliared	13

MADNESS

Landscape With Dead Beloved	17
Tablet VIII	18
[Fragment] that moment in the wildlife management area	20
[Fragment] *in the wildness she created valiant Enkidu*	21
Walking the Dogs Between Blizzards	22
[Fragment] that moment when in my head	27
[Fragment] that moment when he knew	28
[Fragment] that moment when someone opens a can	29
[Fragment] Bardo. The poet speaks	30
[Fragment] that moment when you discover the word	31
[Fragment] The canine neurologist's office in Albany called	32
Realization, With Dead Beloved	33
Witch, 12:48 am	34
The Question of the Epic Is: How Do We Go On, Heart Open, In The Presence Of Death	35
Poem for the Beloved, Eight Weeks Dead	36
Conservation Area	37
[Fragment] That moment when you are the animal	40
Deadweight	41
[Fragment] that moment when I gathered you up from the ash	42
[Fragment] Some bonds, some loves, are so deep	43

AMONG THE SCORPION PEOPLE

Iliad in the Wilderness	47
Hyperopia	48
[Fragment] That moment when you realize you have become	49

Apex	50
The Sleep of Bronze	51
[Fragment] That moment on the way out into it	52
[Fragment] the world swallowed him	53

UNDER THE MOUNTAIN

Tunnel	57
Go West	58
[Fragment] Those terrible minutes coming down	63

THE GARDEN OF JEWELS

[Fragment] …Twelve leagues he traveled under the mountain	67
Green Mountain Prose Poem	68
Surface Tensions	69
Moosalamoo	70
Ignition	71
Home	72
Embers	75
Freezing Up Blue	76
Coyote Tori	77
New Year's Turn	79
Shattering the Blue	80
What the Forest Said	81

SIDURI

"Mourning Is A Love Song"—Blurb From A Dead Beloved	87

FERRYMAN

Timeslip: How Epics End	91
Urshanabi	94
[Fragment] that moment in the estuary	95
Pinks	96
Enjambed Ghazal, Second to Last Line Unwritten	97

WATERS OF DEATH

[Fragment] that moment when the owl you just passed	101
The C Word	102
Poppet, Unmade	103
Drowning	104

Mamquam	105
[Fragment] that moment when dusk falls	106
The Waters of Death	107
[Fragment] I could not think you were dying	110
Miles	111
[Fragment] that 3am when you Google search	112
Crossroad	113

FARAWAY

Rope's End and the Text Extant	117
[Fragment] that moment when you ask	118

THE GATE OF GRIEF

Nightwalk	121
Hallows	122
Bennett's Meadow Was Not A Dream	123
Turning	124
Ghost Walk With Dead Beloved	125
Time, with Dead Beloved	126
[Fragment] And then there's the single one of his hairs	127

FLOOD

The Mountain That Isn't There	131

TRIAL

Trial By Dream	135
Fog of Sleep	136
Songs for the Dead Beloved	137
[Fragment] Surviving the beloved is a praxis of waiting	138
This Dream Is About You	139
Gilgamesh and Hercules Run Hell for Breakfast	140
The Fires Underground	141
Fire	142
[Fragment] that moment when there is the smell of toasting	143
[Fragment] Seven loaves of bread	144

WATERS OF LIFE (THE WASHING PLACE)

(Reeds)	147
Rescue	148

WOLF, WITH DEAD BELOVED	149
WITHOUT EVEN THE CONSOLATION OF REEDS	151
SNAKE BY THE WATER	152
THRESHOLD, WITH SHUGOREI	154
LAZARUS IN MUD SEASON	155

URUK

[HE WHO HAS SEEN EVERYTHING, I WILL MAKE KNOWN]	159
AT WORLD'S END, THE CITY WALLS	160
ACKNOWLEDGMENTS	173
SWEET NOTHINGS	175

Unfamiliared

We don't live anymore in the time when there's that woman who lives way up on the mountain in that crazy, ramshackle house made of equal parts barnboard and found-objects, surrounded by broken-down stuff and overgrown wildflowers;

the woman who has an animal that is of her and with her and for her and from her, but even more clearly and unnervingly not of human origin at all and she is of it, with it, for it, and from it;

we don't live in that time anymore, and so when we meet her and her familiar, we both recognize her and cannot;

she isn't always a crone (though she might be, and eventually will be), she has high-speed internet run up the side of that mountain in fiber-optic cables, she works jobs that do not require her to speak of teams or corporate family, she buys in bulk, buying time during which she does not have to come down;

her animal is always with her and humans always know that to her they are not as interesting (only a few of them don't mind);

we know tales of the woman whom no one could marry and call her a virgin goddess and tell about how she sicced hounds on stalkers at bathing-spots, but the woman, she's just as likely as not to come to our beds, it's just that she won't be there in the morning because we are too loud, too extraneous, to cope with when fresh from the liminal, where she is all animal and awash in relief from her human form, and besides, she has to go home and feed her familiar, who wasn't very comfortable on your bed anyway;

we know just enough of her still that when we meet her with her animal we envy this thing we can see and feel but not understand so we do our best to demolish it, or hunger for it and try to stand close to the heat it throws but know always that the flame is not of our own generation and sooner or later resent it;

we do not live in a time when there is that woman, the witch, the shaman, the *inugami mochi* and her animal with whom she is one being in two bodies;

we fear them because if they are not magic or divine, they must be doing something we are not, and so we warp stories to say the *inugami* was created by us by being buried alive or tortured to death, as if bonds of this kind could be forged in a crucible of anything other than unguarded, unequivocal, inhuman love that sooner or later costs everything, but always sooner and during is the key to everything;

we do not live anymore in that time, and so when that woman's familiar dies, we do not know how or why it is that she does, too, because after all, when a person dies, it's not something that can happen over and over, daily, hourly, riven by minute and over a human span of decades, is it, unless you're talking myths; it's a final and singular thing, death, we know this, she knows this, the riven one whose grief we can't fathom—

after all, she lives there, in both the life and the death, in all times, and that is why she is not of ours, and why she cannot even bleed or eat when the *inugami* is gone, her circulatory system has turned to ash, her organs shut down;

that pulsing you see in the inside of her wrist, it's misleading;

it's the familiar's heartbeat, not hers, pounding drums from an echoing cavern deep, deep underground, where Ereshkigal's hooks are in the walls and there are many wrong turns, and where at the still and dusty center, a single, sickly pomegranate tree grows stunted from uneven rocks.

MADNESS

Landscape With Dead Beloved

Sometimes, flame.

               Wildfire.
    Brush,
         soil itself,
even snow,
            even the ice

burned in searing instant.

    Flesh from bone,
bone from coherence:

    this rounded pile of ash,
spinal cord still articulated.

Tablet VIII

May the trees and the rocks and the trails
        mourn you

[...]

May the paper birches strip themselves of their skin
        and hobblebrush rip itself up by the roots
            to lie down in weeping cradles
                of meadowsweet and dog-toothed violet
                    in mourning

May wooden bridges hurtle off foundations,
        mourning the lack of your feet
May the beechnut keen itself in two and cast forth a grove of cedars

[...]

May quartz extrusions shaped like dragons
        crack themselves open in the shape of your name
            and weep ten thousand tears of garnet

[...]

May the deer, the moose, the wolves
        mourn you
May coyotes fill meadows with lamentation for you
May the chickadee whistle your summons
        forever mourning that you do not come
and may every dog lie down and howl

May every forest that lacks you
        turn the billion scents of the world to one
            and sandalwood become the breath
                of every living being who mourns you

[...]

My Onyx Anubis, my Friend:
        I will fashion nothing for you
            with these empty hands
                but a place to carry you always

[...]

The skin of the lion will smell of you
        and the wilderness echo with mourning

[...]

(Like) eagles' wings over the beloved's face,
        my soul's mourning

[...]

King Gilgamesh

[FRAGMENT]

that moment in the wildlife management area where I took him
tracking for his last time: just me and his empty leash tracking
rabbits, wild carrot, deer sign, cold wind, distant gunshots, bindweed
and goldenrod, leaves going over to yellow, even red already. Clouds
pressing. Stumbling as he did on tussock after tussock, following his
faint track by memory since there's no sign: here the beloved's feet,
here the beloved's nose, here the beloved's remaining joy, here, this
empty leash, chest, survivor, brother-bride, corpse; here, this wind
and the sharp edge of cold coming in to stay

[Fragment]

   in the wildness she created valiant Enkidu   *born of silence*

      his whole body shaggy with hair   *he had a full*
          head of hair like a woman

        his locks billowed in profusion   *he ate*
         grasses with the gazelles

         jostled at the watering hole
                    with the animals
        his thirst was slaked
                    with mere water

        becoming aware of himself
he sought

                      a friend

Walking the Dogs Between Blizzards

    We walk, Gilgamesh and I, in preparation for the storm,
twenty-five inches predicted. Weeks below-zero and chilling winds
solidified feet of snow already fallen; finally,
    we can walk, skating across surface, only occasionally breaking
    through. Gilly runs for sheer pleasure, throws himself forward,
compensates with sheer velocity
    for uncertainty of ground. He hurls his body into space, ahead,
ever
    ahead; plants his face suddenly into snow when he falls. He
always comes up laughing, black fur dusted white, ears crinkled. This is
what dogs do. We haven't walked enough lately,
    snow too deep, crust too unreliable. I want to check on the
beavers; it's been many weeks
    since we've walked enough, in the back field and the woods by
the stream. So we pass
    Shalom's grave, a circle
    of stones and a Japanese Maple surviving it's second winter
under heaps of snow. In a few months, the leaves will appear, scarlet,
determined; yellow Narcissi will rise around the small tree to shout
aggressive, happy color at the sky.
    I invite the dead on my walks. Gilly leaps
    gratitude for our Northwesterly direction: behind the house,
no stacks of wood to fuss with, no barns in which we do mysterious,
officious human things
    —sorting recycling, trying to get the damn mower to work—
    no mailboxes to check, no boring cars for grocery shopping.
To the Northwest, only trails; the ones I built with an ancient pair of
garden shears, with bleeding, blistered hands while I grieved
    Shalom
    one tough, fibrous goldenrod stalk at a time,
    for miles. Gilly bounces me repeatedly; I shove him off, but he
doesn't stop, because I'm laughing. He knows that if a joke is funny the
first time, it's even funnier the next
    twelve times. He bounces, I laugh. He bounces,
    I laugh. This is what dogs do.
    We pass the old shed full of ancient farm equipment abandoned
by the hippies who built our place, the Boyle Farm family

before them. Manure spreader, enormous steel carrot washer, old
sleds, hay rakes with snapped handles, detritus from ramshackle
greenhouse. The piles irritate. We have history enough
 of our own, the interesting nature of the machines
notwithstanding. They threw nothing away, ever, and everything left
is broken, it weighs
 a ton, it has to be dug out of the ground where they let it rot.
One person's history;
 another person's litter. We crunch through the stretch of
trail that is marsh in spring; quails and pheasants nest there, sudden
explosions of wings when we pass
 the Christmas tree I dragged out to the property line,
barricading the gap that invited hunters from the next farm. Gilly
pees on it obligingly. Do not pass, no killing
 here, the yellow snow says; this land is a territory belonging
to the living, and to certain ghosts who are in that condition because
of the likes of you: you who are not welcome
 here with your gun and your beer can and your 'he came out
of nowhere,
 he died within minutes.' Here
 is what dogs understand about time:
 now. Or:
 forever away from now. For a year and a half I have walked,
understanding what 'minutes' means to a dog who is dying,
 alone. *Good boy, Gilly*, I say. *You have a nice, big pee right there.*
There is other pee around the Christmas tree, too; coyote, probably.
Good coyotes. You mark that territory line. Mark it
 well. We pause
 at the choice of trails: left into the lower field and a short-cut
to the beaver lodge, or straight toward the woods and stream, the
long way 'round. The sumac canopy over the track into the woods
beckons. Gilly looks at me, I look at him, and we break
 for the woods—I lecture his back: *stay off the ice!* He dances
ahead, happily
 ignoring me. At water's edge we see tracks and follow them
to summer swimming hole, a convergence of streams. The small pool
is frozen
 now, swift waters bubble under ice. Dry Brook—named
for miles of course that run underground—rises ice-cold, even in
August, from the South. From the East,

Unadilla Brook runs warm through the swamp where trunks of dead trees rise gracefully, sometimes home
    to eagles, herons, hawks. The tracks to the pool are large, but dusted with new snow; I can't tell who made them. Gilly tests the ice on the swimming hole, of course. I cringe
        at creaks under his feet, his spread-wide toes, the light from below makes his webbing purple, his claws scrape for purchase. Convinced he will break through,
    knowing he won't, I have to look away. I inspect the deepest mystery track, shout: *I thought so!* Gilly hurries over to see
        what's so exciting. *Look*, I say, squatting down, pointing into large pad impressions and the outline of claws. *Bear.*
    Gilly plants his nose in the print, snuffles enthusiastically, inhales snow, sneezes it back out in an explosive
        burst. His eyes water. I laugh, so he does too, ears crinkled, teeth half-revealed. He slaps my knee with his paw. Another good joke. This is what dogs do. Back through the woods,
    we skirt frozen stream, through maple and birch, under giant sycamores' thick, mottled, white trunks rising like enormous
        bones overhead. The lodge is a white heap at a bend in the stream. Ice unbroken around it; no tracks. Utterly silent. I wonder if it is warm
    in there, under the ice and snow, in the muddy heat of bodies, snacking on stored branches. I guess it is, if you're a beaver.
        We back up away from the water; I don't like to intrude
    at the lodge for long. We never see them, but we eavesdrop on summer cannonballs into water, felling of trees. We spy on smooth impressions of teeth everywhere. We admire amazing feats of engineering. We sneak glances, as unobtrusively
        as wonder allows. Above the lodge, the field we mow into a rough circle each summer is a smooth, white ballroom floor now. Gilly races to the center
    and does a gavotte.
        I used to come here with Shalom, renovating the abandoned house; before trails, before carrying furniture, boxes, his body, shovels to dig
    his sudden grave. One day, Shalom and I stretched out in this wildish ring of field grass and milkweed, goldenrod, buttercups. We cloud-busted

    together, for an hour; each chewing a piece of grass, on our backs. My arm around him. His head on my shoulder. His heart beat on my ribs. He smelled like grass,
    Shalom did: even in winter, he had a grassy smell. I buried my face in his fur during February cabin-fever and March doldrums and breathed deep summer. Gilly's smell is more floral, especially
    when he's hot. His little armpits reek of flowers. His breath smells like mushroom soup. Right now, he has his first cold, so his nose is running
    in the chill. The sky has a laden, leaden look all too familiar this winter. The light the soft-focus of imminent storm; edges softened, outlines blurred. It's warmer than it's been. Gilly and I follow tracks,
    rabbit, then squirrel, chipmunk, deer. Rabbits and deer move in purposeful direction. Squirrels, chipmunks, mice, and dogs run in circles; they leave intricate swirls and knots of passage in the snow. We follow them all, winding
    home past sleeping pear and cherry trees, cluster of pines, winter-berry brilliant red, we avoid hawthorn spike, drink land. Near the house, mulberry trees tangle messy and delightful. In summer, their berries turn bird guano the most alarming shade of fuchsia.
    Shalom
    goes and lies down in his grave. I wonder if it is warm in there, under the ice and snow, with his buried bed and his toys and his
    emerging bones. I guess it is, if you're a ghost.

    Ducking under tree boughs, a treasure: *Gilly!* I point. He looks up at the branch above my finger, where a single, frozen apple hangs. Apple,
    one of the first English words he learned. He apple-dances every summer, tossing them over his back and leaping to catch them
    before they fall. His first autumn, he ate so much fermented fruit he got drunk. Gill Farm Apple Wine, we laughed, sitting at fuchsia-streaked picnic table under mulberry. Gilly sits
    for his apple. I jump for it, hand him treasure he carries inside to thaw by the wood-stove. Later, he'll throw it around, smear it all over the couch and the floor. This
    is what dogs do.

The storm arrives. I eat a Chinese pear, lemony sweet burst
on my tongue, a summer taste. Outside the window, fine,
small flakes fly in diagonal sheets, the kind of snow
that isn't fooling around. Shalom's grave looks snug, and
lonely, a white heap beyond glass walls. *Come in*
by the stove, love, if you want, I say, through ice, through silence.
Gilly, in his bed by the stove, looks up at me, bleary, already asleep.
I wink at him. He goes back to sleep. The wood hoop is full, the
covered shed stocked,
the stove-flue seems to be working again. I have candles,
kindling. My favorite tea, cream. A working flashlight, another pear
in the fridge. Vitamins, St. John's Wort, good dark coffee. Andres
Segovia and Yo Yo Ma,
split pea soup. We are settled,

in for the duration.

[FRAGMENT]

that moment when in my head
                        the needle in his vein

fixed instead of ending him

[Fragment]

that moment when   he knew

      when he cried   no

            don't take me from her

[FRAGMENT]

that moment when
someone opens a can of Campbell's Golden Mushroom Soup
the exact smell of his breath

[FRAGMENT]

Bardo. The poet speaks
of the intermediate state,
the liminal stage after death
but before the spirit leaves.
Still entwined with the old life.

How am I supposed to live in a world
that includes your last breath in my palm?

[FRAGMENT]

that moment when   you discover the word
shugorei

  the spirit who stays to watch over you
             standing always

  slightly behind and to the left
  your face my scotoma

       your presence
 at my back

[Fragment]

The canine neurologist's office in Albany called, you have an appointment tomorrow.

I keep telling them, but they won't believe me.

Do you want this, the vet tech said kindly this morning, offering me the receipt for your cremation.

On Hogback Mountain's peak, I tried to claw the box of ashes open and failed, nails torn. The wind would have taken us both.

Today I cut five inches off my hair

Realization, With Dead Beloved

And then it comes: the knowledge
that nothing bad can ever happen
to you now, there is nothing left
to protect you from. Half a turn
now, this planet without
beating heart. His face
my scotoma, the only
constellation.

Witch, 12:48 am

for a moment
I smell the wet spring night

the way you smelled it
rich with meaning

before it goes grey again
inexplicably dead as you

The Question of the Epic Is: How Do We Go On, Heart Open, In The Presence Of Death

How stupid and ineffectual, love that can't stop death.
How valiant   and beautiful.

Poem for the Beloved, Eight Weeks Dead

Meniscus, tread: soft
lest surface break and spill
oceans beneath. Once
I wrote water strider words
on that hazardous, bright surface;
now, there are few. What's tread
is tread silent. A laugh could break it all.

Conservation Area

Remember the time we went all the way out in Podick and managed to actually and truly lose ourselves where the trail complicated, tangled, seemed apparent enough to draw us forward but left us in shoulder-high grasses and treacherous buried fallen logs invisible in undergrowth, tall dead trees sentinel bones overhead, and we wandered around in circles, knowing we were going in circles but refusing to believe we wouldn't find our way clear; like the soldier in Passion in the Desert ("you can't get lost in Egypt, there is the Nile and there is the sea") we were lost, and like him, too—once he got to the djinni stones, anyway, and the jaguar, and the oasis—we didn't mind because we were there together, laughing, at rest always in the us, certain that regardless of what was happening, all was well.

Remember?

I did that tonight, thinking, in the same onslaught we had of vicious deerflies and insatiable mosquitoes, deer ticks everywhere plucked and dropped, plucked and dropped: *at least these fucking parasites can't touch ghost, my love—*

Remember the time years before that, when some shitheel shot at me (probably one of the guys attached to the fish farm the next acreage over that got busted and shut down for killing herons, piles and piles of heron corpses discovered behind their greenhouses, a heron mass grave), the bullet audible beside my head, tearing out a hunk of the tree behind me, probably drunk, probably thinking it was funny— and homicidal with protective rage *(what if it had been you?)* I chased the shooter until he was clearly gone, called the cops when I got back to the road, got bounced between the Sunderland and Amherst departments while they argued jurisdiction, none of them wanting to go miles out onto the conservation trails, me saying, with a patient and calm 80-below wind chill in my voice regardless of summer: *you want them shooting hikers on posted land, fine: make up your minds good and firm, though, what you're prepared to accept in your town, once you decide whose town it is, of course,* and of course by the time they got someone out there it was an hour later, no trace, and you were so bored with the whole stupid thing.

Today, an owl, a barred owl, an unusually big one, woken by my
deerfly-switch, dove and coasted the clearing past me, stopped in
a raggedy fir woven with dogroses up twenty feet, and watched
me while I watched it, camera forgotten: crows became hysterical
and starting shrieking about criminals awake in daylight, up early,
goddam owl, and the owl, with a sort of shrug, flapped slowly up and
through dense hemlocks to some quieter neighborhood.

Did you see the owl, love?

Or the three deer, two at field-edge, belatedly noticing me and
flipping alarm-tails, leaping high arches away into the woods, deeper;
later, I came right upon one and she shrieked, actually said *eeeek!!* I
think, and how your laughter—your laughter would have—

Of course the night heron, posing on the sentinel bone tree:
remember when we watched a black-crowned one at Cranberry Pond
in Leverett for a long while and oh, how it sang: we couldn't figure
out what it was but fascination held and held us, we looked it up later
and now I know what they look like, now they are known by Us, and
it posed, and immediately I said *night heron, look*—but then: *maybe, it
might be a bittern, I can't tell, and it won't sing anymore.*

I was sort of lost as we were that time, but I didn't care: the last
mile out from the disintegrated trail marked only by coyote, deer,
following their scat and prints, a doe not a buck (*see love, no spurs*),
coyote not so huge, but not so small either, a good sized one, trail-
marking with piles you would have found interesting, rabbit fur and
bone fragments mostly. I wanted to find us, where we were that time.

I was tired and you weren't there, but at least the bloodsucking
parasites couldn't get you, it was only my own eyes at risk of getting
whacked with dogrose thorns, corneal scratches avoided carefully,
it was only me clambering over sunken trunks hidden by tangles
of wild rye shoulder-height, only my hocks tearing, only my hair
snagging in caves of staghorn sumac and mountain laurel,

all of it choking, all the way through, overtaken by young trees and
deadfall,

until the only way out was to close my eyes and go animal, go ghost
with you, and follow the sense that isn't human at all back to where

I started, pulling ticks off my shirt and twigs tangled in my hair and withdrawing a thorn from under the skin once back on the trail, thinking:

such an odd place for sudden wilderness: right up against everything else, a small but quicksand wild full of fairy mounds and temporal shifts, we always liked it here,

thinking

it might have been a bittern

thinking

we should get some fried chicken—you'd like that, wouldn't you, love?

[Fragment]

That moment when   you are the animal   in the trap
        saving   the last bite   of everything
                yourself excruciate   unsaved

Deadweight

The massage therapist's hand
on the back of my neck, my body
spits memory—visceral, and what
the psych people call *intrusive*:

yeah, it's pathological, all right,
that the infinite Beloved's head
should loll in my hand like that,

pulseless and cooling.

[FRAGMENT]

that moment when I gathered you up from the ash

    your bones the weight of driftwood

        and feathers: my brother-bride

            I am eagle's wings over your dead face

my soul's mourning,   my brother-bride

                        and so   I carried you

      so light as to barely be there   in my arms

should not my cheeks be emaciated, my expression desolate?
should my heart not be wretched, my features not haggard?

should there not be sadness deep within me?
should ice and heat not have seared me?

my friend whom I love deeply
he the wild ass who chased the wild donkey

panther of the wilderness
he who went through every hardship with me

the fate of us all has overtaken him

[Fragment]

Some bonds, some loves, are so deep the two cannot be kept apart,
even by death:

like quicksilver, they will pool back together across any barrier,
no matter the cost to the nature of things.

Among the Scorpion People

Iliad in the Wilderness

It's not the worst thing, is it, to pretend
that if I leave, he'll be there when I return
from epic, mad quest? It works in the stories.

Retinas   purged   of his   going dark—

Visiting the edge of a mountain hanging over Pacific fjord,
orcas herding dolphins herding smelt, sea-lions and eagles
hovering over the face of the (water) (beloved), waiting their turn,
I teach The Iliad:

and darkness veiled their eyes.

Again and again, darkness veils their eyes
and the palm of my left hand holds
the beloved's last breath, a burning city:

This story is so violent, a student says, appalled
by the specificity of bodies in death.

Hector for the moment, I take off my helmet,
place it on his head. His eyes fill. So much water.

It's such a tender gesture, the student says.
That scene on the battlements. His humanity!
How it ends! This isn't right.

Hyperopia

On neutral ground of no-memory, surcease of expectation
that you will see this wild beauty of western mountain,

eagle, bear. Broken in half, I become someone else:
thousands of miles just enough distance to see clearly.

The center of gravity shifts from the space between us
to inexplicable solitary core, hollowed.

I can move, toward vanishing point: I can find you
there, can't I? Vanished. I will find you. Far. Away.

[Fragment]

that moment when you realize you have become a person who cannot let a sleeping dog lie

      unbearable, their terrible vulnerability

                    you wake them   to prove

                                        they are not dead

Apex

Six orcas in Howe Sound, breaching
far enough away to see only fins: *come close
as dream*, I plead, but they do not. This morning
I got up, made coffee, and went back into the bedroom
to wake you, expecting your lazy-morning laugh
because I had to come get you, sleeping in, sort of,
one eye open, listening, knowing I would come spoon,
enticing love: of course, the bed was empty,
you're dead, ash in a box, and the orcas,
unheeding, did not bring you back to me,
carried in their mouths gently, from that world
to this, spat upon shore at my feet, laughing.

A man next to me, Squamish, praised recovery:
it's good that the life is back in the sound, he said.
Yes, I answered, and we watched, pointed, watched,
happy. He introduced himself. Larry. I told him my name
and we shook hands. *Nice to meet you, cuz*, he said,
and then he called me cuz several times, making me
one of them, and I was grateful, moved. After a while,
he slapped me on the back and wandered home. Others,
Squamish in cars, trucks, welcoming the orcas, smiled at me;
Larry's approval a handprint on my back. Breaching, tears.

Gilgamesh, I said, and wept. *An orca brought you home.*
But they didn't. Not today. Only in dream. In life,
it was the heron who wanted to get next to me: *look at me!*
he kept saying. *I will bring you close. Look at me,
alive! alive! alive!* The feathers on his breast angled
in the precise arrangement of your ruff.

The Sleep of Bronze

Iliad in the wilderness, for the third time, all bardic cycles
cycle in threes: six months gone and down we drop
into the sleep of bronze, night closed on our eyes.

A student writes: *I finished the Iliad today
because there's no way I can keep
this up for a week. I see blood
when I close my eyes,*

and crushing empathy
drops its wine-dark depths—

the eyes, the eyes, it's all that darkness veiling
all those eyes, and if I could I'd crush her to me
in some kind of mortality-defying embrace,
Gilgamesh at world's end, but not failing this time:

*awake, awake, Gilgamesh,
for seven nights and six days, and death will die.*

Instead, loaves of bread, made stale
by the passage of time uninhabited
by the beloved. Page upon page
of blood. Flashes of beauty so fierce
new pages fall into our hands, crisp
and blank.

[Fragment]

That moment   on the way out into it
        when from habit   you ask empty air:

                do you have joy in your pockets, my love?

and as he did, the air shimmers with it, alight and laughing,
            and so are you,

                        so all is right with the world—

                                    until.

53

[Fragment]

the world swallowed him   and all the light went out

UNDER THE MOUNTAIN

TUNNEL

Without that green   tapetum   pair
coming at me   through the dark

what use   this mountain   wearing such stars?

Go West

> *One league he traveled…Dense was the darkness, light there was none.*
> *Neither what lies ahead nor behind does it allow him to see.*
>
> *…the North Wind licked at his face…*

Gilgamesh spoke to Utanapishtim, saying:

if you could hear it   this screaming

                 would leave blast craters

> *[…]*
> *Enkidu, my friend, whom I love deeply,*
> *who went through every hardship with me:*
> *the fate of mankind has overtaken him.*

[…]
I have named the Jeep Utnapishtim.

Gilgamesh in the front seat, riding shotgun, a box of ashes.

[…]
Niagara Falls, and a walkabout to stretch and see the falls: the place itself is toxic, bad-smelling, but the power of the Niagara River washes it away. How I would have loved the place five hundred years ago.

> *[…]*
> *Six days and seven nights I mourned over him*
> *and would not allow him to be buried*
> *until a maggot fell out of his nose.*
>
> *[…]*
> *Three leagues he traveled…Dense was the darkness, light there was none.*
> *Neither what lies ahead nor behind does it allow him to see.*

[…]
Lake Erie. Pushed longer, and here, hoot owl welcome following a doe and twin fawns who fearlessly examined me as I examined them. How he quivered around the edges of that deep stillness in the seat beside me.

> *[…]*
> *I have been roaming long trails through the wilderness.*
> *How can I stay silent, how can I be still!*
> *My friend whom I love has turned to clay;*
> *Enkidu, my friend whom I love, has turned to clay!*
> *Am I not like him! Will I lie down never to get up again!*

[…]
Mirror Lake, Wisconsin

A green and rolling land, each rise and fall taking me by gentle, cornsilk-scented surprise. I'd imagined it flat, but it undulates in fertile green heaves, ocean waves of clean air. Cut grass. Corn. Woodsmoke. More corn. Otter prints everywhere in the sand around the lake: an otter rave clearly happened here.

How you would have loved this, I say aloud.

This Ho Chunk land is called "Ishnala." It means: "stand alone."

> *[…]*
> *That is why I must go on, to see Utanapishtim whom they call The Faraway.*

[…]
The Mississippi River's enormity. Pushing Utnapishtim up rougher hills and asking more of the engine, people less friendly, one small place where I stopped for gas practically a ghost town, shuttered. Coldness radiating from the few people I saw: broken receipt machine at the pump and no one in the attached store, locked up tight.

No wildness anywhere. Just cloudshadows on wind-whipped oceans of corn, or concrete.

Minnesota. A dead prairie dog on the side of the highway says changing ecology.

[…]
Sioux Falls riddled with drugs, but still somehow seductive. Black Hills at the edges pulling me in; the smell of dust and sage and heat. Falling away, everything from before.

A loop past Deadwood and into Lead—vertical climbs and falls so steep and narrow I had to stop and turn around, go back, Utnapishtim's transmission weeping, pulling the trailer.

[…]
Hundreds of miles through Badlands like the crumple of sheets left behind by torrid giants.

The ponderosa-scented air, sharp-shadowed edges of Black Hills lit gold.

I camp in a petrified forest, agate bones. A dog named Sadie guards the campsite.

[…]
Nine leagues he traveled…Dense was the darkness, light there was none.
Neither what lies ahead nor behind does it allow him to see.

[…]
Wyoming. At first the sensation is that of being an ant, but gradually, from smallness, expansion to fill the available space.

Dead Horse Creek, Crazy Woman Creek; names to rival South Dakota's *Two Bit Road* in Deadwood.

Pressing on from Sheridan to Billings, Montana. Transmission seems okay now, but a hard day on Utnapishtim the Jeep.

[…]
Eleven leagues he traveled…Dense was the darkness, light there was none.
Neither what lies ahead nor behind does it allow him to see.

[…]
The first 100 miles of Montana at late-day sunset, then dusk, was lavender. Stranger than Wyoming. Gentler-edged drumlins and high downs, gold purple blue green.

At Little Big Horn, a million crickets. A violin-symphony over the still field of ghosts. Somehow, full of life, replete with time.

Slept beside the Yellowstone River.

[...]
I went circling through all the mountains, I traversed treacherous mountains,
...that is why sweet sleep has not mellowed my face,
through sleepless striving I am strained,
my muscles are filled with pain.

[...]
The Continental Divide is behind us. Only one semi on fire on the pass. The caravan of limping engines crept by without incident. Missoula.

[...]
Missed business opportunity, Wallace, Idaho: "Circle one: I (did/did not) piss myself on Lookout Pass."

Also, fuck you, Idaho panhandle. Seriously. No one mentions that after Lookout, there are approximately 12 more passes before you get to Washington. No, they're not as big. Talk to the smoking brakes and redlined transmission about it.

In Coeur D'Alene, a mechanic says Utnapishtim's doing fine, just hot.

Snoqualmie Pass is closed for rock blasting.
I'm in a hotel in Ellensburg.
Sometimes you have to just call it a day.

[...]
Eleven leagues he traveled...Dense was the darkness, light there was none.
Neither what lies ahead nor behind does it allow him to see.

[...]
Border crossing. It's all border crossings from here.

Vancouver.

Farther.

North.

The Sea to Sky Highway put on a lightshow-sunset for me, coming up (and down, and up, and down) to the farthest west.

The Faraway.

Utnapishtim gets a tune up and a rest.

[FRAGMENT]

Those terrible minutes coming down Greylock Mountain in falling dark, and their mad conviction: *we can outrun it. If I just drive and drive—to Vermont, to Ripton, to Battell, right now—*

we'll go back in time. He'll be so strong again. We'll have the wolves.

The Garden of Jewels

[Fragment]

>...*Twelve leagues he traveled under the mountain, and then it grew brilliant.*

Witches do not stick; their temporal slides move everything, see?

>*[...]*

>...*it bears lapis lazuli as foliage, bearing fruit, a delight to look upon....cedar...agate...of the sea...*
>*lapis lazuli, like thorns and briars...carnelian, rubies, hematite, like emeralds...of the sea,*

>*[...]*

>*Gilgamesh...on walking onward, raised his eyes and saw...*

The garden.

Sure, that one.
And that one, too.

The Green Mountain National Forest. Eden. Oasis.

Who told you there was a difference? The question is

>when.

Green Mountain Prose Poem

I won't mention the moose; she's too large, too definite for this poem which is more on the scale of the two efts I saw at roadside, ember-bright and uninteresting to the dog. We argued all the way up the next hill about the relative merits of juvenile spotted newts vs. bear scat, quick forward motion, the smell of nearby sheep: he won, though I did my best, even softly prodding a small, bright body right under his nose to produce a lazy, intriguing wiggle. Nothing. The dirt road passed under our feet in a startling onrush of miles, the sheep stared stupidly and complained incessantly about their jobs while the dog, somewhere deep below his fine manners, considered with lust how easy it would be to eat them. A flower not truly a daisy but some essential caricature of one stunned me into a momentary lapse of capacity to contextualize, but the dog dragged me on and hill after hill of them emerged from the illusion, a carpet of singular experiences, each different, not one more valuable than another. This poem isn't massive flanks and fly-covered musculature straight out of Neolithic swamps, certitude and patience in long-lashed pools of time; it's passing miles, passing hours, observation of the small details while the large context is kept to the self, close. Not the moose but deerflies, culverts, vetch; dog pushing ever ahead, the dirt passing beneath until a roadside red under flowering grasses reveals wild strawberries everywhere: small, ripe, sweet.

Surface Tensions

The words return, thunderhead incantations; rain begins.

Clavicle. Foamflower. Stone.
Rivulet. Trillium. Femur.

Each drop tastes of iron, I am drunk with green;
clambering down with the water to moss-softened edges.

Scapula. Gaywing. Waterfall.
Whitewater. Club-moss. Occipital bone.

Each drop hits my skin, slides down my blades, is absorbed.

Water pools in hollows of trees, of clavicles;
petals turn upward to catch and hold it.

Philtrum. Starflower. Eddy.
Meniscus. Forget Me Not. Pelvis.

It is never entirely clear to me
whether I am swallowing rain
or rain is swallowing me.

Swallows dive into dusk surface, pluck water-striding words, one
after another, for sustenance: the dives are sustenance, too.
Radial pulse. Loam. Spillway.
Dog-toothed violet. Ripple. Throat.

Indistinguishable, the cell-walls between us.

Hobblebrush. Sonnet. Iris.
Body. Forest. Animal. Sky.

Moosalamoo

Twenty miles through twenty-thousand acres of Green Mountain National Forest.

The dog and I explore, scaring up quail: they startle us with explosive wing-thunder. We watch chipmunks and peregrine falcons, find an isolated and well-cared for camp at the top of a long and nearly vertical side trail, an old and water-distorted moose print.

Beeches turn the air gold, the sky shades from robin's egg to cobalt with wisp-clouds stirred through it. Birches in bigger and healthier stands than is usual grow large and straight from boulder-strewn ground. The boulders themselves sport elaborately embroidered moss and fern blankets.

We mean for it to be a short hike, an exploratory foray of the trail mouth for later. The mountain pulls us up, higher up: *look at this here*, it says. *Look here.*

Turn this way, and look at those mountains over there.
Look at these crystalline days of brilliance.
Look how you drink it in, so thirsty.
There's more.
Come a little higher.

We answer with soul-deep hunger.

We wish to never come down.

Ignition

Did I tell you the thing about the coyote concert, the fisher, the dead fawn in the road? Did I tell you about the chickadee tree, an oak purely writhing with hot little brown bodies calling, scores of them, tiny bird upon bird? And how I stood underneath it and said: *chicka dee dee dee dee* and they answered and we spoke back and forth for ten minutes, one after another of them hopping down to the low branches nearest me, peering into my face with cocked heads and shining black eyes curious as they corrected my pronunciation? Did I mention the peregrines, one after another, hunched shoulders and strong necks, sailing almost as close to me as the bat who took a mosquito from the air in front of my face, so close my eyelashes were ruffled by wingbeats?

Did I tell you that the maple in front of that house on the back road into town, the yellow house, that '50's atrocity with the fake colonnades, is the best one anywhere? Did I tell you how thick the red spreads there; gobs of red, spatulas of red, slapped gleefully onto that luxuriant bough-canvas, crimson and fire-engine red with sharp orange outlines, and how I keep wanting to stop and take pictures, take leaves, take something of it for permanence or memory, but it's all going too fast, I can't keep up?

Did I tell you the highest mountains here are all calico now, every one of them, the peaks a few days ahead of the lower slopes, the slopes ahead of the valley floor, but all of it rushing tinder bursting into flame and burning itself out as surely as the wood I'm burning in the stove from trees ringed and dried standing for ten years, then cut and split to burn fast and hot, kindling, kindling everything, and it's all going so fast I am afraid to blink, to miss a single breath, look, look now, it's so fast, don't stop looking, did you see it? Did I tell you? Look—

Home

White pine cathedral cliché overhead, giving way to deciduous forest: I worry about porcupines all the way to and from the fallen-down house. Keep the dog near me.

After, we go to the general store for chocolate milk and freeze-dried liver. Leaning on the counter watching dust motes, I mention the hike, the comparative absence of deerflies on that trail behind what used to be my family's farm. Dick wants to know if we went all the way to the bluebed house.

> The ruin, you mean?

> Yep, he says. Before it fell a blue bed stood in the abandoned downstairs. Everyone called it that.

> Yeah, we did go up that way, I say. It's beautiful up there.

Now it's all down, and nothing blue is left. Just lathe without plaster on jarring slants toward the sky and all of it, even the roof, arching from the cellar.

It's not sad; it's not anything to do with what it once was. It's a new thing now.

> We kept watch for porcupines, I say.

> They're pretty much gone, Dick says, patting my dog's head, which is unabashedly plonked in his lap for reasons of mutual adoration.

> Gone? They used to be a plague here, I say. My wolf-hybrid had a vendetta: we had to plier quills from his throat almost every summer day. Sometimes twice if we didn't keep him in and he had the rage on him. He was determined he was going to win one day.

> Some dogs are like that, Dick notes. People decided the porcupines were a problem. They'd eat the hoses from your car radiator, then your barn for good measure. Someone imported fishers twenty or so years back. Now the porcupines are dead, and so are most of the quail, and a lot of other things.

A lot of people's cats, too, I say. I didn't know someone brought them in on purpose.

Stupid to bring in a big, alien predator like that, just let it go, Dick agrees. Stupid. But now their numbers are going down. They ate themselves into starvation. New things will come in. Maybe the porcupines again. Things have a way of self-correcting, he says.

The wolves are coming back, I say. Maybe they'll eat the remaining fishers, give things a chance to rebalance.

The dog comes around the counter, sits on my foot. I scratch his head.

They gave my mother a hard time in the barn, I say. Ate the reins, bridles, everything. Hassled the horses, too.

Oh yeah, Dick says. They'll do that.

One time, I tell him, she was walking and there was a porcupine sitting in the middle of the dirt road, maybe eating something, I don't remember. She picked up a log, wound up, and slammed it across the bridge of the creature's nose like a Fury; vengeance for every quilled dog, every shied horse, every damaged stall and chewed door and consumed saddle. The log turned out to be rotten. Disintegrated into a million pieces. The porcupine shook off the dust, stared at her like she was crazy, kept eating.

We laugh and laugh, picturing her slinking away, stymied.

That's a good story, Dick says.

It's not what it was, this forest, but it's not sad.
It's a new thing.

Minks and wolves share the wood behind my house, otters and coyotes avoid us as a result. A mile away, there are fishers, but not here because of the wolves.

Here's how it is: people are deerflies on the mountain's skin, a small irritant plague. We drench in citronella oil, head out into clouds of them, irrelevant. We worry about quills. The mountain floods, freezes. Generations pass, billions more than ours.

Porcupines are still here, or if they're not they will be again: we'll slink away home, stymied, floors eaten away from under us when we're not looking.

We'll fall into the cellar and reach for the sky having become something entirely other than what we were: ours are the smallest numbers of all.

Generations pass. We keep the dogs close.

Embers

Equinox spent with chimneysweeps, then gathering
apple boughs fallen and dry from old orchard's edge
for kindling: apple wood smells better than any other
in sharp, autumnal air. The stove is crackling now,
hoarfrost forming on grass still green and tasty.
My hands smell like wood-smoke, reminding me
of someone I once loved, I can't think who: maybe
all of them in wool sweaters, under down blankets;
every autumn love now fallen, drying on the verge.

Freezing Up Blue

Stay the course. The river freezes
from the bottom up, on this mountain;
static slush grows like coral,
whole barrier reefs of it.

It's something to do with copper,
the cyanotic water skin; too cold now,
to remember what it was.

Come by the stove, sit.
It gets easier, after some time.
The feeling goes. The parts
you lost fall off. After some time,
you'll notice it's been years
since you missed them.

You'll say: our rivers
freeze up blue here.
Come, sit by the stove.
Here, the djinni
freeze up blue.

Coyote Tori

A sharp, bright, blue day, ten degrees and golden white. In the woods, beeches lining the trail make rhythms of a million rattles; icefalls from high boughs to deep drum of crusted snow add bell and bass sounds.

An attractive pool of far off light draws us deep off the ski-pressed track: the dog and I struggle through sheets of shattering crust sinking to knees, thighs, shoulders. A natural clearing holds us in the cold, immobilized by gold and white and blue, by cracking pines and the diamond glint of everything under the sun.

Back on the trail, we follow coyote tracks running parallel to the pressed snow.

The crust is unbroken, it was a lightweight animal. I cannot tell for a while if it is a solitary coyote or a pair; finally, I find their entrance. It was two. They came up from the river gully far below, went miles back into the woods using the human-pressed-trail to make their passage easier.

Gilly finds scat: mouse remains deposited in a clump of indigestible fur and bone. Rabbit tracks are everywhere: maybe some of them in there, too.

I rarely hear them, the coyotes. They do not need to sing near humans, the forest is large enough for their harmonies to remain private.

Missing their music, I stop to listen, and see a gate:

a tall maple has shattered in the cold; snapped and tipped over sideways, splayed flesh exposed to the sky. Its body shapes a perfect A, a temple tori opening onto a short plateau, a steep drop into the river gulch far below.

I call the dog.

We break through the ice and stand at the threshold. On my right, blood from the shattered tree has frozen to a brilliant resin, amber in small crevasses of bark. I take off my glove, put my hand on the smooth effluvium; hold it there until the heat from my body runs sap into my palm, down the body of the gate.

The taste on my fingers is sweet.

This is not the sort of gate you do not go through.

We break through the ice, further.

We step through it.

New Year's Turn

—and then
there were stars;

the red planet
scarlet at the center
casting hot light
through the heart of everything

scathing heat, an eros of light
red and spreading

distant fireworks
announced the turn

and a star streaked across black
under Mars and away
the last of the year
immolating itself
in a final surge
lost in the dark

I watched it go,
blaze out
to nothing—

calendar, losses
turned

to bright, cold sky
and laughing dog
in my arms,

to shuddering trees
and ice-dense winter rivers.

Shattering the Blue

And then, the river broke: vast ice sheets cracked like cannon-fire and sped to crashes in snags and bends, pressed vertical, diagonal, in curves of widened banks funneling speed and frozen mud in deep and arctic torrents.

We heard it go, the immobilized course: heard frozen-up-blue shatter into movement at last. We knew what it meant, and we ran to it, fast as overflown banks and the full press of thawing mountains. The water undercut the snow-crust. We could not go close, the ground was no longer frozen beneath us, but flowing, moving, changing.

We picked a careful trail thirty feet back from the river's violent edges and watched, filled with glee, as stirred as bed-mud long-frozen pulled hot in relentless current.

A small, lithe body emerged from the far bank, skated across the ice, and dove into the melee of torrential ice-break. She swam underwater, rose; stunning navigation of current and floes, ducking chunks of ice far larger than she—and all, clearly, for pleasure. A mink, dark chocolate and supple; a tiny otter surfing ice for joy. Another. Then another, more: we gasped, watched, empathically ducking chunks of ice hurtling past. Shivering though they did not, we laughed: that hurtling river—hot, bright bodies celebrating inevitable thaw—

What the Forest Said

Tell me.

>   Which part?

All of it. Any of it. Just—something vivid.

>   -

>   I was walking.

Yes?

>   And there were two deer.

Whitetails?

>   Yes, whitetails, flashing alarm. They heard the dog. I didn't tell him; he was looking for a good stick, something nice to throw. The deer flipped their tails and danced away. I could see reflections of yellow beech leaves in the eye of one of them, turned toward me: she was that close.

-

Tell me another.

>   I don't know what to tell you.

Please.

>   -

>   Bobwhites.

What?

>   Six or seven of them, exploding from the underbrush with wing-beats so loud I ducked. The dog ran so fast he ran right out of the orange t-shirt I put on him to differentiate him from bear.

Bear?

>It's bear season. They're shooting bears.

Oh.

>He treed them.

The bears?

>The bobwhites. They were furious.

I bet he was proud.

>Very proud.

-

You're going to leave, aren't you.

>Yes.

Soon?

>Probably. There isn't much left.

There is. There could be—

>Shhhhh.

-

One more. Tell me one more.

>-

>Once I walked into the woods and there was only one way: further in. I walked and walked, and I was fierce and beautiful and brave and resourceful and I had many adventures, but I was getting tired. Very tired. I couldn't walk any more, finally; I couldn't be fierce and beautiful and resourceful and brave any more. Also? I was bored with myself. With all of it. I dug a fire-pit, lined it with stones. I gathered wood, and made a fire. I was so hungry, but I had nothing to eat and I was too tired to do anything else, so I sat by the fire and watched the flames. I figured I'd probably die of starvation eventually, but really, the flames felt good and I couldn't think what else to do. A stag came out of the

> forest, walked right up to the edge of the fire across from me. We looked at each other for a long time, and I thought: how beautiful. After a while, he lay down across the fire and split himself open, his blood steaming in the coals. I ate his flesh, and was restored.

That didn't happen.

> No?

No.

> -
>
> -
>
> I saw a peregrine eat a bat today.

Yeah?

-

-

You're going, aren't you.

> I'm going.

-

> I have an idea.

Yeah?

> When I go, just look away.

-

Okay.

-

-

Now? Should I look away now?

SIDURI

"Mourning Is A Love Song"—Blurb From A Dead Beloved

"Dear Jessamyn,

Once one enters the universe of Grief, you learn to live there because you will never live entirely in any of the universes that define our lives. But it can't be any other way. Grief is the most agonizing and enervating expression of love, because the soul for whom and to whom we give the love is not there to receive it. The soul we loved is no longer with us in his familiar form, but the relationship we have to that soul is stronger than ever.

There is an essential cruelty to life, which is that the essence of living is relationship, and the essence of relationship is love, is soul-connection, and when death ends the relationship, it does not break the connection, and thus we grieve because we are left with shadows of the connections but the pulsing blood of the connection has been stilled and now we express our love through grief, and grieving simply does not end.

[…]

… soul relationships are of another order of being, especially if one knows the soul not as a thing, or a place but as an energy that is uniquely you, an energy that, when shared with an equally unique energy, enables you to know yourself in ways not possible before.

I say all of this to say that…grief will not diminish with time…grief will only intensify and deepen…how could it be otherwise when souls interpenetrate?

[…]

Ah…the suffering that is held in our muscles, bones, marrow, and in the very cells of our uttermost being.

But it is not only what we have suffered. I am convinced that suffering is handed down through the generations like the heirloom no one knows what to do with but no one can get rid of until it reaches one person in the 10,000 year old chain that goes all the way back to those ancestors who survived the last Ice Age, and that individual has the resolve to say that the family's suffering stops with me, and that person looks at the suffering, dares it to do its worst, and endures the accumulated pain of generations upon generations, and one day that person is cracked open, and the suffering pours out of muscles, bones, marrow and cells, and the ancestors find the peace that has eluded them, some for 10,000 years.

So, yes, when that happens there is an imperceptible change in the structure of the universe.

[...]

I should say, death still pisses me off.

I love you."

—Julius Lester

FERRYMAN

Timeslip: How Epics End

I.

Temple   broken,
spine   a snapped
reed,   mourning:

Gilgamesh leaves the pool behind,
snake long-since departed
with consolation   prize

and youth a bundle of reeds
turned kindling   broken
    against a careless knee.

Fire: extinguished.

II.

I'm getting ahead of myself.

Mortality's neck
was to be crushed
between stigmata hands,
remember?

We thought we could out-walk it,
death, covered in ash, rending
our robes, great fistfuls of hair
severed on the ground.

In the end, even consolation
snakes away, a thread of blood

in water.

III.

When Aesclepius first came into the underworld,
lifted us off the meathook embedded in our rotting back,

carried us on despair-dark paths of stone dripping cold,
opened our chest, removed the silent heart, and breathed

life back into it, we were disoriented: Wait, which story
is this? We asked. What is Aesclepius doing here?

Anyway, it beat, it desired, it loved
this world again, that kindled heart,

so we wrote The Ascent, wondering why no one
ever tells that part; how brutal it was for Inanna,

or how beautiful, how dangerous an animal
hope really is: it never occurred to us

that Aesclepius himself would sink a dagger
into the heart he so laboriously resurrected,

and unceremoniously
send us back down.

IV.

It never occurred to us
the stone would be rolled away

and light would fill the Lazarus cave,
blinding; that we would emerge

blinking and there would be a single daisy
so perfect it hurt; that we would be torn,

right there at the cave entrance, limb
from limb by Maenads or Romans

or someones, we still wouldn't be able
to see very well and would remain

not quite sure what was happening,
it would just be that everything

went asunder and there was
a lot of blood and pain.

V.

I think we are supposed to be talking about Urshanabi?

VI.

Anyway, it never occurred, any of this.
This is not a true story.

Walking west in madness, walking east defeated,
full of meathook holes all over: the short hours

in a garden made of jewels in between.
In every passing corvid his iridescence.

His face. The only constellation.

Urshanabi

Sharp wind and cold, tumbleweeds
composed of bracken, early heather.

Curled into the stabilizing trunk
of his body, skeletal remains

shift and creak. How is the day
we found the otter scat composed

entirely of fish scales three years
gone? Tree susurrus answers *yes*.

Branches, spine, groan. Pain, drop
by drop. The Ferryman's hands

move it all.

[Fragment]

    that moment in the estuary
           all our familiar scents
                  alder leaves drying
                        yarrow
                                snapdragon
                                rosehips
                                chickory
                                            pearly everlasting
                                          pearly everlasting
                              everywhere pearly everlasting
unfamiliar: seagrass
              mountains of cedar all volcanic and glacier
                                    the moment of his death
                                        how hard he fought it

Pinks

The shallows-rocks are swimming: body upon body
    a cold press of backward glance—
how this beak tears flesh
    still living, how your mouth
shaped my name. How once light sank
    a clear shaft deep, and what we saw
though we weren't supposed to.

Going swimming? That devastation of smile.
    Hmmm. I answered: *Glacial runoff, zombie-fish—*
how much will you pay me? Your startling blush
    payment enough on those cheekbones.
How I dropped pants, shirt, waded, dove.
    Current fierce. Cold lung-stopping.
Body upon body, memory is a cold press

desire sometimes indistinguishable
    from glacial torrent, cerulean and ice.
How when I came out gasping, you gave me
    your sweatshirt, looking down at the ground;
my skin risen to mountain peaks, snow-capped.
    How I never touched you, not once, not intentionally,
though fuck, it's all I wanted in a dying world.

Their skins peel off distorting bone
    before they are done with them.
Your mouth shapes my name. Water on the slopes
    of these pressing bodies, mountains upthrust;
convection of currents, magma beneath.
    How I loved you in the shallows.
How I saw you in the depths.

Enjambed Ghazal, Second to Last Line Unwritten

Tonight the rain is salt Pacific: I can't help but pull back.
No going back, once tasted, but pulling salt-thick petrichor

from asphalt shoals, I'm trying to turn the boat, the undertow.
What I could give you—nothing I could give you that you don't have.

Everything in this ocean, spilling into me, in response.
Nothing you don't have. How you left the shore and touched me, shaman,

with your beautiful combs. How desperate and soft my love for you.
How many death-fathoms can one creation goddess survive?

Down here, even the seals and whales vanish. Sedna left to bone.

WATERS OF DEATH

[FRAGMENT]

that moment when the owl you just passed
        who was apparently busy disemboweling a mouse

turns into a baseball bat to the back of your head,
      as you are walking away
           and you stumble, baffled by impact,
                    then shout at the bastard:

what the hell did I ever do to you? I'm on YOUR side, and the owl,

                  now on a low branch, just says
                  death! death!   and you say

            enough! enough already! just stop it! blood

                      trickling down
              your neck, into your shirt,
                      soaking
                    everything,
                everything red.

The C Word

When it comes for you, after taking so many of yours,
everything goes bright: there are questions.

They resolve down to one.

See, suspicious cells can only mean all in, and eagles.
Bears. Blank pages. Relentless immersion, the wet.
What is given. Right now. It helps

if you relax, she said, patting
my abdomen under the blue paper skirt.
No shit, I answered, gritted. Do you find
that feasible when someone is holding a knife
to your cervix? She had the grace to laugh
before cutting, and the wait. One time,

I was in the underworld and I saw
a pomegranate tree growing stunted
from uneven rocks: a drum beat shook
the cavern but it was not his heart,
it was mine, jagged and uneven now,
a ghost-pulse, each beat a desperate, failed
seeking. Another time,

I fell through the surface of the earth and landed
inside a jaguar: she smelled of flowers and we were one
being in two bodies. I had never been so happy. For decades,
I searched for that smell—finally, I found it: we were one being
in two bodies, and for a long time. I had never been
so happy. Every second, I knew what I had.

Is it a gift when it's mortal?
It destroys the world, loss like that.

Her answer, eventually, was: you're okay
for now. My answer, eventually, was: yes.

POPPET, UNMADE

When I set the two pieces gently on the water
      —a human figure front and back,

threads cut and pulled, separated from cloth
      and intent, all contents let go into waves—

they first float on their backs, in lazy eddies
      circling back to me, then begin to sink,

to tumble and fold. And when the Mamquam current
      takes them at last, a hundred swallows come,

scoring the surface with psychopomp wings:
      they bring tears, finally, released

by necessity. Back to the dark place of origin.
      They gather it all up and take it away.

Drowning

When lungs fill
        thrashing bodies
disappear   black water
       a slow deafening
the loudest drum
rippling everything
that is left

        <<<< >>>>
        <<<< >>>>

        <<<< >>>>

this wasn't
supposed
to happen

      what now?

      it gets tiring
      making decisions
      like these

<<<< >>>>

      one thing
      about Sedna
      down there
      on her throne
      of bones

she never makes you
do everything alone

      her winding hair
      is all up in your business

Mamquam

Linden hint and wet stone. Driftwood
elaborate and white as bone, smooth as defeat
in my hand. Before you leave, don't forget to ask
the river: how many, beauty, have you killed?

[Fragment]

```
that  moment when dusk falls      four-legged and low to the ground
           scent a precise mathematic:      aspen (drying)
bear scat (blackberries)        sedges (high tide)
            human (beer-urine)       miles (covered fast)

            searching      still no trace
      human        forest        stumbling bipedal and dilated

                                            shadow-catching
calling      calling      screaming      into chasms
                                                      gulches
vocal cords      torn and bleeding        Us
                                              the knobbed arches
                of spines        aligned each to each
                   a single breath         animating us both
```

THE WATERS OF DEATH

I.

      His hands drew magma, fire   rising, following
magnetic forces   ore-driven by pain
    I took to   engulfing him   quick
and quiet,   so deep there was   no swallow

     see   the line between   dying and resurrecting
is molten   when a whole world   is reshaping itself
    words like   *love*, like *please*   have no bearings
you know   what we give   cracks us open

II.

    It's strange, dreaming; the Beloved's guts in our hands, smooth as river-obsidian: extinguishing and kindling, breathing him into song, breathing him in, tearing out   our own guts, slippery and gray, casting them for augury of hope on desolate ash.   The bears, the dragons, the bursts of linden off the river winding white tendrils   around our bones, which are also trees: how the stars became his face, how flares   both solar and nocturnal send indistinguishable shocks of light and pain, all heat.   We owe a cock   to Aesclepius, for sure, friends: the poor man has been listening   to all of this all this time,   and no one wants to hear what you dreamt last night.

III.

Give me some   kindness,
    anything—small
is fine—   to go on?   Silence.

IV.

It's a series of experiments, this chronic
re-invention thing: at a certain point

hypotheses are proved or disproved.
Perhaps who you are now is a person
who walks through open doors. Or
perhaps you are the door. The hand
slammed in it.

V.

    Doors slam, mercenaries
        exsanguinate. What have you
to offer? Work harder. We are
      an extractive technology.
    Marrow is next. Lie down.

VI.

Staccato gasps. She writes:
    "Prayers. More scans. Tomorrow."

She can't breathe now, is bleeding.
    Her spine bends, arches, collapses.
A sudden dowager's hump, death
    curled to spring under her thinning skin.

Tumors are growing
    she writes   and new ones
forming   resistant to chemo
    trying   something else now

VII.

You spend 72 hours firing people   when you have already been fired.
We call this   *personal regret, budgetary issue.*   One of those
peculiar waking-dreams   when the brain slides sideways,
    fantasy   more real than life   for the urgency in it:

    just go home, drive back east. Unspool all those miles
    and at the other side of the world he's just waiting
    for you there, alive!

This was all a regrettable business decision,
sorry: a silly mistake.

VIII.

Maybe you are the door. Maybe you are passing through.

Unremarked, shadows of leaves on tree-trunks white as bone gut you. You gather it all up, smooth as obsidian. Cast it on ash for augury of hope.

[FRAGMENT]

I could not think you were dying.

It was not part of our vocabulary.

Miles

Cormorants, gulls arguing in the dark—
salt on my lips a necessary magnet:

oceanic, we called the air
on Mount Greylock,

your last dusk, falling down,
a sliver-moon and nearby star

burned purpled into retinas:
every dusk to come that last one.

[Fragment]

that 3AM when   you Google search

    why would a creature's bones become heavy?

        nothing to explain

                his
                sinking

CROSSROAD

At the joining of the Mamquam and the Mashiter, failure:
where I live now, this deep-cold channel, laval evidence
of cataclysm everywhere. This is me without him, now.
This cut. This world. This face. Riven. Eagles tear what flesh
is left. Even the new-grown, still pink and thin. Soon now,
there will be only bone. Clean and bare as driftwood.

FARAWAY

Rope's End and the Text Extant

      Utanapishtim spoke to Gilgamesh, saying:

      You have toiled without cease, and what have you got!

    Through toil you wear yourself out, you fill your body with grief,
     your long lifetime you are bringing near (to a premature end)!
Mankind, whose offshoot is snapped off like a reed in a canebreak…
          No one can see death,
        no one can see the face of death,
       no one can hear the voice of death,
         yet there is savage death
          that snaps off mankind.

           Gilgamesh said:

             […]
  The gate of grief must be sealed up with pitch and bitumen!

[Fragment]

that moment when you ask

wait, *which parts are true?*

and the answer is *the rain* *bears* *salmon*

and the dog

I keep telling you

this is a story about witches

and madness

The Gate of Grief

Nightwalk

Yeah, so, the sadness comes
around that bend in the Mamquam,

full of silt and glacial. All I need
is that low sliver-moon and a man

who can stand a little emergency;
better yet, some Nina Simone and the dead

returned—I don't recall giving permission
anyway, which makes it criminal homicide,

or at least theft. He's calling, you know,
under that moon, and I can't get to him.

In my empty hands, I have two real things.
The musculature of joy. His last breath.

Hallows

Remembered with the same viscera,
the dead and the past. Futures, too:

your fur under my hand, your hot breath
in the palm of my hand, Billie Holiday

will be on the radio, years gone veils
one torn from the next and fire

consuming the slowest deer,
the one who went back.

I dream I'm floating, out there
in all that wet: oh, you peeled me

like a mango, and I dreamt of foxfire,
drowning in it, Sedna-bones knocking

into beaver-pantries, submerged rocks.
Maybe there's a way back from it,

a way up. I don't know what it means,
that rocking silence of waves, matte silver

like mercury, like a shark's eye, flat
and appraising, unlikely as any simile

recurring from poem to poem, finally
inarticulate as everything else.

Something bloomed every time I gazed
at your animal face—imagine that:

something inside actually blooms. This one
true thing I know. Every time. Now and then.

Bennett's Meadow Was Not A Dream

We take the path dead center through severed cornfields; it's hunting season, the woods to be avoided. The wind rockets, a deafening ocean in our ears. Dog sprints, top speed, ears laid back, spine curling and uncurling like cheetahs, after the stick I throw with the wind to increase distance: it flies apparent miles, into explosions of starlings blackening the sky. A pheasant feather attaches itself to me. I hang on to it tightly as everything vibrates parallel to the ground in the onrush of air, even us. The sun heels to our right, herding us so our shadows elongate across low-cut corn stalks. Dog bangs his stick against the stumps as he walks, thumping rhythmically; a November heartbeat.

Turning

Gone, gentian fringe
and liquid—slick, now,

treacherous frozen
and memory
hard as stone.

Orion's Belt points.
There's Sirius, dog star
bright in a new year's sky.

What use, these lights? We were stars
once, in our own private firmament.
Now, chiaroscuro sky-bowl pours out,
black and bright as he.

GHOST WALK WITH DEAD BELOVED

This moose track, look,
still filling with water;

how we stalked that one
in Ripton for a silent mile

only to lose her across a pond,
ripples fading, leaves going still

across the water. Painted turtle,
look. We—I mean I—mean you

no harm: you'll find the right spot
for those eggs you carry, go now

and find it. Miles now. Jump
this fallen trunk, scat-marked

by coyote, oaty horse piles
beyond. Miles more, worrying

about you pushing too hard.
Later, I'll fix us something:

turkey. Gruyere. Some red-bean
treat, rice glutinous and sweet.

Your acolyte mouth
takes mochi communion.

Time, with Dead Beloved

Now I move from place to place
where he isn't   dark matter absence
a vast,   visible weight   pulled
with my body

      this verge
verges into that pullout,
      towns, roads, years
in temporal scramble

     witches often have trouble
with time   every morning's first act
on the knife-border   between consciousness
and soul   is reaching

     each hour awake
Rilke's panther   pacing
hour to corner   to hour to edge

     to verge   to car
to walking   where
    he isn't   to driving again
anywhere
        until tired
   enough
some air   can get in—

      until on 116,
   a motorcycle accident
enters in,   rushes down

     through tensed, arrested muscles,
stops my heart   thundering

    and is gone.

[Fragment]

And then there's the single one of his hairs that comes out of the printer, attached to the latest poem.

FLOOD

The Mountain That Isn't There

> *They made a large (canoe) (raft) (raft of canoes tied together with cedar rope) and when the waters came, they tied up to the peak of (Garibaldi) (Mt. Baker) (Icecap Peak) (Mt. Cowichan).*
>
> *This is how the People survived the Great Flood.*

In winter, it appears to hang in space: one vast glacier diamond, ice-white on black vault of sky. Her Milky Way diadem, his face suspended. Fixed for all time. Or not. That sharp peak we threw the longest cedar bark rope around. To fix ourselves. Suspended.

Thousands of miles gone now, ice has come again. The thud and crack of it, the long, cold wind.

I track the absence of dogs: how quickly they disappear. A tether, a run gone, and no trace now of the pale-eyed mutt, wolf-like, who spoke such dangerous violence until I learned her name and sang it out, perplexing her with an intimate song of sweetness: I would whisper-sing her name, songs of her ice-pale eyes and their glinting fire, and her snarling terrors would turn to aching whimper, a plea for me not to pass by. *Come back,* she would whisper-sing around long canine teeth, *and sing to me that I am beautiful, again?*

A pool of summer heat, light: morning, and how easily we could speak, hear, sing.

Stone and snow-glow, ice-reflected Pleiades in Ripton, in January, in 3AM silence but for the squeak of sub-zero crystals underfoot: how tightly wrapped we had to be to survive knowing this precise cold and silence, this sky on the ground: how beautiful it was, how our hearts beat in unison.

Smoke, now, and ash. Cremains: I read about wildfire smoke's effects on the body, how particularly bad exposure results in pneumonia-like symptoms, arrhythmias, suppressed immune system, vulnerabilities; how we bounce back pretty quickly, usually, unless we don't.

Night walk in ice-wind so sharp and strong I almost get knocked down: gust upon gust, my skin is burned, chapped by it. I am lifted and dropped.

A lake. A river of fire pouring across it. My lungs are made of smoke and ash. I can't get warm: we are burning up. The garden-claw at the base of my spine screams, metal on metal on bone on ice.

Some things cannot be recalled, once released into the darkness on the surface of the waters.

The dove. The raven. The peregrine sailing.

They do not always bring back (olive) (laurel) (cedar) branch.

Sometimes words. Sometimes ghost.

I am looking for a mountain that isn't there.

TRIAL

Trial By Dream

And Utnapishtim said to Gilgamesh: *to kill death, you must not sleep for six days and seven nights.*

Gilgamesh sat, and put his head between his knees. Sleep, of course, like a fog, immediately blew upon him. Darkness veiled his eyes. We know how these stories go.

Utnapishtim said to his wife: *bake loaves for him, and set one beside his head for each night he sleeps.*

When Gilgamesh woke, he saw how he had slept: the first loaf was desiccated, the second stale, the third soggy, the fourth turned white, the fifth sprouted mold, the sixth was still fresh, the seventh was still warm.

And he knew he had failed.

Listen, my friend, to the dream I had last night,
Enkidu had cried to Gilgamesh, just before he died.

…now must I become a ghost, to sit with the ghosts of the dead.
To see my brother bride no more.

To the living the gods leave sorrow.
To the living the dream leaves pain.

Fog of Sleep

The fog a live animal. Over the banks.
Ice. No tenderness in this world
but ghosts, now, and scythes:
memory. Dream. Darkness.

Recursive tendrils, tender animal
memory fogged by pain, painkillers:
ghost-dreams in daylight, only me
curling over him, a sodden breath.

Curling over banks, live animals
in the fog. Tender leaves, sodden.
Ice on a possum's back. I remember
his rare requests for me to wake.

Darkness. Fog. A possum ducks ice,
sodden. He breathed into my face
when he needed me to wake. Tender.
The sleep of bronze. Night-closed eyes.

Animal ghosts. A mist scythe, memory:
his rare request, tender breath. Wake.
Curling across dreams. Stop playing
dead. Wake now, beloved. Wake.

Songs for the Dead Beloved

1.
It was the bear's face, not the wolf's,
that resembled yours in sleep; down
under the large paw, denned in dreams
of certain unity and salmon—

>   2.
>   so in a patch of late snow
>   my hand melted
>   Neolithic signature.
>   Iceburn language
>   for what can't be

3.
half a turn now, this planet without
beating heart. His face my scotoma,
the only constellation.

>   4.
>   I want the sky
>   to be the ceiling
>   that caught you rising.

5.
Mourning doves. Chickadees. Coyote howls.
Say nothing, please, I ask the owls. I cannot bear it.
In the far west

>   6.
>   restless mountains search:
>   see how jagged and lean,
>   what chasms open dusklight

7.
with fingernail slivered moons
spilling into fjords. Under the black,
sure and fast, an orca brings you home.

[Fragment]

Surviving the beloved is a praxis of waiting.

Waiting is a praxis of madness.

This Dream Is About You

A few months after you died, a Haida orca brought you back
from the depths, mouth gentle, spat on solid ground:
      how we laughed, wept on the shore
and I said *you sank, you sank like your bones had turned to lead*
and you said *not anymore they're not* and *did you see the dolphins?*

You were a cave wall of sandstone, and I couldn't press
close enough, so I put my mouth to the skin of rock
      and you dissolved, pulled back to tunnel;
from that narrow abyss you sent forth a vast, coral serpent
to breathe into my mouth and make of me a new creature.

On the sides of I-80 across Pennsylvania, coyotes: teeth bared
and midsections crushed. Deer with rubber necks, hawk
      catastrophes corpse-strewn—we drive past all of it,
grimacing and surely broken. At the rest stop, a guy says
can you help me, I ran out of gas, so I give him 5$ & a dream

about dreams, not lucid but waking, teeth bared in one last effort
to stop the onrushing grille: sometimes I can still see you there
      riding shotgun, even wide awake, your silvered eyes
slitted against springlight. *Remember having brown eyes?*
To the guy at the rest stop: *yeah, it's a bad stretch of road.*

Gilgamesh and Hercules Run Hell for Breakfast

And I dreamt that under the Hunter's Moon, in snow, Gilgamesh and Hercules, the wolf-dog hybrid of my childhood, ran hell-for-breakfast for pure joy in silver moonlight on white, in sharp, clean cold. The forest bright even in midnight. Wolves were pursuing them, and I was, too, trying to keep them safe: vast joy in their joy, and worry, for Gilly especially, 77 pounds so small compared to the rest. The dogs were unafraid of the wolves, perhaps foolishly: such games they were having, catch me if you can. A dangerous game, I wanted to say, but like them, I admired the wolves, who conserved their energies even as the dogs spent theirs in wild happiness: they were tracking more than stalking, keeping an eye on things. Perhaps alive, perhaps liminal. These things don't matter here. To see these ghost dogs happy, to see them together: to see them race all that silver light on white-laden boughs. To see the wolves' casual following, uncommitted to predation, but possible, always possible. To see the dogs run up the base of a cliff and keep going, straight up; a nearly vertical face and yet they sprinted it, their joy sure-footed as goats, my breath held the whole breakneck climb. Up they went, up to the top, to the plateau up there where some night-hunter with a club was taking swings at them and missing, where the wolves had come around by an easier path but sat now in an amused semi-circle watching the failed swings of another ineffectual biped foiled by canine bursts of zig-zagging speed: the dogs barreled onwards through the snow, their ears cupped forward in laughter, and disappeared, and the wolves laughed, too, and I said *be careful, my loves, oh be careful,* and the hunter threw down his club in frustration. How they galloped in the snow! It came up to my hips, powdery but immobilizing. Even left behind, upright and slow, how I thrilled for them, so vibrant and fearless. Can you call something bravery when the only consciousness is of joy? Look at them go, in undiscovered country, free of all this.

THE FIRES UNDERGROUND

And I dreamt that you were missing—of course, again: I was searching for you in resigned calm, panic built-in now, accustomed to search. A chasm, into which you might have fallen, a broken bridge over which you might have gone. A forest, dark and rainy, whose trails I walked and walked. Mud-slicked ground, and the earth itself porous: a foot or two down, under the wet soil, shifted and shifted again by my hands, fire. Fire underground, everywhere. *Look,* I said aloud. *It's all on fire.* Red embers and shifting magma, humus itself burning, scalding my digging hands.

Fire

And I dreamt that fire took the house and I let it, sitting on the pillows by the window, his ashes in my lap: I welcomed the smoke into my lungs and hoped it would put me out before the flames reached me. Sunlight and clarity on waking, disappointed. A box of ash in my hands.

[Fragment]

that moment when there is the smell of toasting bread in the hall
    and working at the computer   I turn to you and say

I propose some toast!   but of course   you are dead

[Fragment]

Seven loaves of bread

and when I wake
you are not there

Waters of Life (The Washing Place)

(Reeds)

Utnapishtim, at the behest of his wife, told the exhausted Gilgamesh:

There is a plant…like a boxthorn, whose thorns will prick your hand like a rose. If your hands reach that plant you will become a young man again.

So in the water, Gilgamesh opened a passage to the underworld.
He tied heavy stones to his feet. They dragged him down.
There he found the reeds, and although he bled for it, he cut them,
and cut the heavy stones from his ankles,
and let the water send him back up.
He placed the plant on shore.

Haggard, emaciated, filthy, Gilgamesh bathed then, in the sacred pool.

Of course, a snake came to the pool, silent,
and carried off the consolation prize,
sloughing its skin as it went,
eternal youth in its mouth.

Desolate and beaten, Gilgamesh sat down, weeping.
Tears streamed over the sides of his nose.

Rescue

Five a.m. and a great-horned whispers about territories and belonging; full wind eddies and the darkness puzzles. It should be pink by now, where have the mountains gone? For a moment I'm not sure where I am. A ghost in the darkness bows engagingly, coaxing: *please be okay*, it says. Trying. When last asleep I dreamt someone had gone down in the lake. I'd gone down after her, but she was hanging there, vertical, near the bottom, a human reed, heavy as lead. Every time I tried to plant my feet the mud was not solid, I couldn't find anything to push from. The owl whispers, the ghost is gone. The wind stills. I wrapped my arms around her and tried to pull her up: the strength of my body insufficient without gravity. My air running out. There are great-horned mutterings and a dazzling lack of light. For years, for decades, I never admitted needing anyone or anything.

Wolf, with Dead Beloved

A shape, dusk-emerging at river's edge
      look, there, I said, and pointed at her

coalescing in the dim:
      she's so beautiful,

I said, sharp curvatures so strong;
      she's a carving, a lupine emblem

some unseen artist made
      in unforgiving darkness,

so wolf she's almost unrecognizable.
      She's lying down, look, I said,

she's going to stay with us for a while,
      she's so beautiful—

at water's edge, in dusk, a charcoal and bone
      musculature of life.

Isn't it amazing, I said, *how strong*
      the will to joy can be

even when you're dead?
      In the photograph a friend sent

from our day at water's edge, an almost
      unrecognizable woman. S*he's*

so beautiful, I said, before I recognized her:
      who is that in all that light?

Such vibrant musculature, shimmering.
      Look, I said, to some unseen artist

driving even the vital dead to radiance.
      Beloved, I said to the shimmer

vibrating just behind me
      always: *look,* and he did.

Two herons took flight, the wolf turned
    a relaxed gaze and looked,

the herons and I looked, a raven and a bat
    turned, too: *hello*, we said,

I see you there,   so beautiful—

Without Even the Consolation of Reeds

Just for a moment now, that abyss in my palm

before seagrass and cattail without context: place
without memory a bearable threnody,

a salt and green scent.

Snake by the Water

I dreamt the eagles, talking: how the elders spoke to the juveniles at such length, so many things to teach them so quickly, and the teens so rowdy with flight; how I could hear them lose their patience, the adolescents laughing, talking back.

I dreamt snow on the Mamquam, even though it was too early and full of pinks, beak-faces still striving; and I dreamt the convergence of fjord and river, seal-heads in channels between milk vetch hectares, seagrass whipping like a woman's hair in fierce winds. Orca dorsals broke teal water.

I dreamt Fawn Lake, steaming warmer than air and silent.

I dreamt cruelty; one spill after another, an oil slick smothering it all so that no part of that world's spirit was left unbroken.

I dreamt of no return.

I dreamt then that Gilgamesh was with me, ghost but fleshed: this time he got to see the wolf, too, right there on the other side of the river, watching the same heron, the same purple dusk, the same eagles. When she turned and nestled, making a bed in the sand and settled in for sunset there with us, he shivered with awe, with love.

We cannot earn rare and wide open love, it is only given.
When it is given, a healthy animal does not destroy it.

Gilgamesh took me walking, then, around our lake in a dense fog. We saw a snake. I said hi, and he nodded, and on we went, his dapper trot ahead rippling the air, and somewhere in there the fog took him back and I was walking alone, and then I was awake.

No dream, how tears began somewhere near my feet, rising through my bones: how I felt my sternum crack, then open, and then they poured: no dream how they would not stop, how they were for and from and of all of this that has been lost.

No dream the still rope hanging, unswung. The bones of that tree, framing an eye in reflection. So many new trees fallen. So many slung dead on the ground. No dream, the pine and copper smell so familiar, or the snake crossing my path, a young garter, spooked. *Hi snake,* I said, and it stopped, looked back at me: no dream, how we held each others' gaze for a long few minutes, and I asked how the beavers were doing, and the big stuck-snapper Gilgamesh and I righted and saved from a heron waiting nearby, ready to plunge beak-spear into underbelly where the shell is inadequate against anything that sharp.

The snake, tasting my presence on the air and hypnotized by my voice, did not answer, but the lake did: *we are a whole new place in three years, and the same as we've been since glacier.*

Yes, I answered. *Me too.*

I looked up, expecting Garibaldi, but of course he was not there. Expecting Gilgamesh, also not there. These confusions don't surprise me anymore. Sternum cracked, and leaking. So much good, and still: assessing. Assessing. So much damage. This. This broken, too. This. All of this was shattered. And this. A process of uncovering, acknowledging. Trying to set the bones correctly.

A low silver sky, dimpling the surface with rain. I asked the water why. *Why? And also, how? How am I—?*   No answer.

Drought has brought the water lower than it's ever been and I can see more of the bones of the lake than I am meant to see. It is vulnerable like this, even still so deep in the center.

Samhain approaching. The time of ghosts, of passages between worlds.

How he swam in this place. How I swam in all of them.
How love buoys us up.
How leaden we can become, when death is winning and the veils are too thin for too long.

Threshold, With Shugorei

you don't have to hurry love

you don't ever have to hurry

holding the door open, the world that was whole, wide open turning east now

take your time love I'm here

Lazarus in Mud Season

Granular now, this ice, this temperature differential, this oblique control: if I had a god she would be that nervous flicker exploding from thawing hay and iced crocus, she would be the question *how?* now so granular, the big parts answered, each green blade iced and stymied. If I had a god he would be the scent of vetiver and campfire: molecular traces in my body granular now in the icy question *why?* left hanging in ground-clinging clouds of snow-melt, crocus buds under glass. I dream of stags, vast-antlered inscrutable. The muscled shoulders of percherons.

Where am I? the question that changes before it is answered. Some land you occupy, some land occupies you: eagles and seals duck torrential rain, witch's hair thirty meters long outlasts all of us. Symbiotic green, our skeletons. It's the salmon bones, you know, that make the trees so big—

Calcium, magnesium, oily E; ibuprofen ubiquitous and the half life of Flexeril a molecular known, certain as faith. Fire overcomes ice, ice extinguishes: where you are depends on where you have been, shot from this field in a panic of flight. Nerve connections gather in low branches of muscle and bone.

A waking bear pulls a salmon from the Mamquam River, distant. Sucked bones left on altar of root. This body drifts in uncertain flow. A cottonwood snags, fallen giant, glacier-pushed: herons nest there, sharp-eyed and still. The air pours linden. Pollen makes endpapers, chartreuse and brick pools.

Ice-sheathed, spring willows try so hard. Nerve connections fire. A peregrine sails, fastest creature on earth. To be so fast, aglow with sap: *where are you going?* Each next thing, muscle snagged on titanium bone.

It still hurts, you know, resurrection; just less than what came before.

Uruk

[HE WHO HAS SEEN EVERYTHING, I WILL MAKE KNOWN]

Tablet I

[...] granted the totality of knowledge of all, he saw the secret, discovered the hidden [...] He went on a distant journey, pushing himself to exhaustion, but then was brought to peace. He carved on a stone stele all of his toils, and built the wall of Uruk-Haven [...] the holy sanctuary.

[...] inspect its inner wall, the likes of which no one can equal, take hold of the threshold stone, it dates from ancient times, go close to the Eanna Temple, the residence of Ishtar [...] go up on the wall of Uruk and walk around, examine its foundation, inspect its brickwork thoroughly.

[...] Find the copper tablet box, open the [...] lock of bronze, undo the fastening of its secret opening. Take out and read from the lapis lazuli tablet how Gilgamesh went through every hardship.

[...] It was he who opened the mountain passes, who dug the wells on the flank of the mountain. It was he who crossed the ocean, the vast seas, to the rising sun, who explored the world regions, seeking life. It was he who reached by his own sheer strength Utnapishtim, the Faraway, who restored the sanctuaries and cities the flood had destroyed.

Tablet XI

Gilgamesh said to Urshanabi the Ferryman:

"Go up, Urshanabi, onto the wall of Uruk and walk around. Examine its foundation, inspect its brickwork thoroughly—is not the core [...] kiln fired brick, did not the seven sages themselves lay out its plan! One league city, one league palm gardens, one league lowlands, the openness of the Ishtar temple [...] the openness of Uruk it encloses."

At World's End, The City Walls

In March, in knee-deep mudslush and unrelenting gray that mires and bogs, even the body is braced and belligerent. It's the end of cabin-fever time: if there has not yet been a murder or madness, there probably won't be, but there are a few weeks left to tell.

Once we drove to the base of Battell Mountain at this time of year.

A foolish thing, on miles of dirt turned ice-silver tar pit, turned shifting, watery peat bog. The car danced, turned hydrofoil, and I wondered:

Will they excavate us ages hence, preserved
hoar-frost skeletons still hungering for spring?

Let them. We'll make it or we won't.

Shivering their own risks, the birch and beech didn't care: I'm glad I saw them glowing there. Saw their sap coming. Some secrets are worth risking, taking entirely on their own terms; a huge upthrust of geologic shift as purely real as metaphor.

The evidence of lichens.
What willows say at that time of year.
How hard it is to bear.

Then, I pined over cabins without electricity, with composting toilets, Coleman lanterns, and round woodstoves. I used satellite views to see how much concrete exists around them, and how much unbroken green. I craved topographical maps, wishing I had forty-eight thousand dollars here, sixty thousand there: it's not so much, compared with what others seem to want, but it might as well be. I sold some books to put gas in the car to go to AWP to see writer friends, to hand out postcards for my book of poetry that would make no money. I took teaching gigs, freelance edits. Over the years, slung coffee and sold hammers, avoiding entrapment, for better or for worse.

A secret: at AWP, I wanted to ask Anne Carson to sign my
boobs. If *Autobiography of Red* doesn't make a person want
that, seriously, what use are they? If *Glass, Irony & God* doesn't
make her a bigger deal than a big-hair band, what good are we?
I would never ask her really, of course, it would be so rude.
The shit women writers deal with already; we don't need it from
each other—but I wanted her to know she gave me more
than rock stars.

Another secret: at AWP, I totally forgot to promote my book.
Distracted by all the raving beauty, by the upthrust of joy in
those who risk everything for the word, I went around giving
long-missed friends and total strangers tattered, fragrant roses I'd
bought at the T station, and hugging people, and listening to their
lives leaked like so much blood onto the page. To Anne Carson,
I said: *thank you for your writing, which has made both me and my
writing more possible in this world*—and, with the last rose,
yellow and bruised: *this is for you.* I was happy and content
already, to have been able to tell her that.
Her smile was icing.

Home, I took the dog to the park, where he became histrionic because we weren't walking; there was too much ice. We stood around throwing sticks, which of course he had to chase: a stick in motion has laws associated with it—free-range hysteria, automated retrieval, patterned responses—but steady forward motion is better, so much better.

I share the unease he had with standing around in groups. It's dull, and invites trouble. In March, motion is pent in us. Penned. He was always glad to see other dogs, though, as long as there was movement.

So many unbroken miles of his youth, my mountains; these given over for something too domesticated for comfort, but lacking all comforts of domestication. This is how we lived then, at the end of a long spell of wintering over lean, not yet clear of it. A storm coming in. The working assumptions that didn't work. The howling wind. Slush knee-deep, mud-stained; everything looking shabby.

If we're to be so much alone, I felt, so much by our wits, better the wilderness, the uncomplicated forward motion. Further up. Further in. Beech secrets. Moose prints in mud, so fresh they are still filling with groundwater. A Milky Way so close you can roll in it. Three a.m. walks, bumping into bears in a full dark of fog: everyone hissing with surprise, then backing away, affirming good intent with noisy, false good cheer. Carrying on in the dark, each to our own purpose. Musk of each other still lacing the air.

White-out on the drive home from Boston, the selling of books, the slippery rink of dog-park hysteria. A short walk around the wild little lake, iced and slipping. Wet.

A secret: I kept thinking *your small hands, precisely equal to my own*. I kept thinking: I haven't really been the same since Adrienne Rich died. I missed my chance, somehow. So many things I wanted to ask her about, to hear her say: what was it like, what were you like, as Grandpa's student at Harvard? Did he see you as he saw me when he gave me a hammer, a bag of nails, a stack of wood for my sixth birthday, in spite of his generation and the rules about girls? How did you break free of the legacies of generations, their terrible weight? Richard Wilbur, Anne Sexton, all the rising stars of Twentieth Century canons just-forming, their trajectories drunken and death-pursued? How did you become kind and generous, and remain so? What protected your ferocity? Now there is no one to answer these things but me. But us. I kept thinking: maybe that's what it takes. There being nobody left.

The dog's bones creaked. We went inside after a mile, plastered with thick, sopping flakes. They obscured the greying of his muzzle, turned his age-whitened eyebrows fanciful. We were neither of us ingénues for a good while already, if we ever had been: we just sometimes wished there had been a little more comfort on the way. More open adoration. A little less burden. One thing about growing older: we do learn to put more things down. To stop lionizing the bearing of unbearable weights.

In satellite view, that part of Vermont with the tiny cabin and the Coleman lanterns looks like what you'd expect to see further north. It says: *shhhh*. It says: *come up. Further up. Further in. Don't look back. Shhh.*

A secret: I live for that voice.

Might die for it, too, one day. Dunno. It always seems possible, it's so easy to make a mistake in the mountains, and mountains do not afford our mistakes. Worth risking, though. And it seems a hell of a way to go, since we have to: by exposure, most likely, though preferably by catamount. Sometimes, during that year in the forest, it was all I could do to turn back, once I started up: there was no part of me that wanted to return. The dog anchored me. His hunger. His need for my life. My care for his comfort. His life.

It's possible there are wolves around Townshend and Newfane, where that little cabin with the lanterns is for sale for forty-eight thousand dollars, right at the edge of unbroken green—though it seems unlikely so far southwest, New York and Massachusetts infringing just fifty miles down or over. Maybe, though. Maybe wolves. They are recovering from us.

Once, still south of Montpelier, reeling from the fresh vision in my high beams, I said to a rest-area guy: *is it possible that I saw what I just saw? I dunno*, he answered. *What'd you see?*
A wolf. A giant. A myth.
Yes, he said eventually. *You did. I see them, too.*
We shared in the secret. He told me they eat at the local dump.
Adaptation, he said. *It's a bitch.*

It was a cartoon, an archetype of a wolf. All ruff and black and green tapetum and teeth. Cleaning up after us.

Environmental Services, we call janitors now.
I didn't know what to think about this. Wolves living off our trash.

> A secret: in the north, there were lots of them, but they didn't need humans in all that unbroken green. We saw only their prints, their scat, their trail blazes. We heard their songs, if we were lucky. All the coyotes shut up instantly and listened, too, when they spoke. The dog—oh the dog, trembling from flews to tail: we vibrated with want of wolf. Drunk with scent and song.

People feel they must pull something other than all of this in from outside, to have wonder. Some narrative thread that departs entirely from the text-extant.

Why? What need of invention? Especially in March, when we have worked so hard to get through. The forest has given more than rocks stars and gods. *Shhh. Come further in. Further up. Listen.*

At the beginning, and at the end: there are the foundations. The city walls.

See, we'd gone home, when we went north. We found a falling-down 1830 farmhouse in the woods just a mile from my family's old place, now owned by Middlebury College and maintained as part of The Bread Loaf Writer's Conference, for which Grandpa was director for a quarter of a century. I was formed in those woods, and my nanny was a wolf hybrid named Hercules. He taught me the best of what I know. His favorite lecture-subject: porcupines.

We found the 1830 farmhouse's owner, drunk on his home-brewed beer: arranged to renovate his falling-down place in exchange for cheap rent. Moved in. Bleached the walls, ceilings, floors. Ripped out rotting flooring, fixed it. Painted. Scraped and dragged through somehow, patching and sealing and sanding and hammering. We learned to glaze ancient windows, their glass gone liquid and drippy.

> A secret: you have probably figured this out, but when I use the pronoun "we," I almost always mean "me and the dog." Or for those long years I did, anyway.
>
> The royal "we."

In the farmhouse, there were brown widow spiders. A lot of them. Also, the heating vents to the second floor had been ripped out to heat the cellar, so the pipes wouldn't freeze: the cellar walls had missing fieldstones so big I could climb through their absences. The heat poured out the holes into the Green Mountain National Forest. These were insoluble problems, in the end, but for a year, it was good.

> A secret: I don't want to talk about the spiders.
> The stones: I did what I could to patch and fill or cover
> the holes, but the heat from the house mainly warmed
> the woods. I liked the idea of this, particularly when it
> plunged to 40 and 50 degrees below zero and peregrines
> fell frozen from the sky, or when the snow got to be five
> feet deep and the deer fell exhausted from wading. But
> the bills. You can imagine. Did you know the venom of
> brown widows rots the flesh around the wound?
> Once I watched a fly consumed from within by that acid.
> It writhed. Desiccated. Collapsed inward.
> Was rolled and saved for later.

For all the rest, we rigged solutions.

There was a lot of bleaching mold, and spray-foam. Patching of mouse-highways. There were moose; in the yard sometimes, grazing the low branches of the apple tree by moonlight. There was a river behind the house, another beneath it: the former I splashed in with the dog, the latter I shored up, rebuilding channels of stone to run the water through without pooling, spring-house-style.

There was an epistolary romance that was enough to carry me through the isolation, and a deep and intimate relationship with the hardware store at the base of the mountain. A brief and disastrous foray into three-dimensional dating, with tenacious consequences of stalking that took more than four years to shake loose. Minks by the hundreds in the East Branch of the Middlebury River behind the place. White-tails, everywhere, thundering and trumpeting. Fisher cats. Bobcats. Bobwhites. Corvids and falcons. Wild turkeys. Coyotes and wolves, in adjacent but separate territories. Hunters' stories—around the wood stove in the general store or in the junk-food aisle of the gas station market at the base of Route 125—of catamounts, seen from hides: scrapes and scat that might be, could be, probably wasn't, but once, but last week in full daylight, but maybe—they spoke in hushed tones, and only to locals, about these cats. Didn't want anyone to come looking to shoot them.

There was our forest. Bread Loaf Mountain, and Battell. The whole history of my generations, there in the cardboard boxes in the Town Hall records room: deeds. Transfers. Ends. Facts to clarify the mud of biographers' hyperbolic chambers, their cabin fever associated with commodification of all things Frost: Frost who for thirty years was my grandfather's best friend, my grandmother's lover, my mother's confidant and compadre, the ghost-presence I knew well enough even as a ghost to know that he was nothing like the stories told and re-told about him until they became more real than the real man. The slant-light, gold and dusty, of his cabin. The unyielding comfort of his Morris chair. The unending fictions of curmudgeonly Santa; how each of his poems is actually about death.

> A secret: hobblebush blooms the size of dinner plates.
> More: there is a heart-shaped spring bubbling just below
> Bread Loaf Mountain. Also, trillium. Halfway up
> Battell, in June, you can find a deep snow-bank
> remaining under a thick and venerable old pine. In
> January, at two or three in the morning, the cold silence
> is so deep, the dark so complete, I could wear the
> dazzling Milky Way as crown, hear its rustling fingers
> comb through my hair.

At the end of that year in the forest, we'd gone home when we came back south, too. Got work, after too long looking, in the town where I grew up: so many who want to be here; all smart, most talented. Three hundred, five hundred bodies competing for each job. The visiting faculty gig got us rental of a house by a pristine lake, a backup water supply protected from human interference. Clean. Spring-bubbling. A Victorian cottage, damp and full of flying squirrels, but also gracious and full of hope.

I taught Plato, Rachel Carson, Gandhi, communicating climate change, genetics, populations, politics, critical evaluation of sources, unapologetic love of the life of the mind, Citizen Kane, the Ramayana and Sita Sings the Blues, a blitz of poets almost all of whom are alive and writing right here right now, the Epic of Gilgamesh: read them, listen. Listen. Speak. Listen again.

> *Find the copper tablet box, open the [...] lock of bronze,*
> *undo the fastening of its secret opening,*
> *take out and read from the lapis lazuli tablet*

At the end of the first semester, a student gave me a letter, in a sealed envelope marked DO NOT OPEN UNTIL AFTER GRADES HAVE BEEN SUBMITTED. She said to me: *I didn't know it was possible for there to be a woman like you in this world. Now that I do, it is more possible for there to be a woman like me.*

> A secret: on the way home from campus that evening, I
> sobbed and sobbed.
> Gut-punched.
> Happy.

Students have said a lot of nice things to me over the years, and I appreciate all of them; what we do together is hard and beautiful and dangerous, like mountains. It's nice when someone says thank you, when you have worked hard to simultaneously blow their minds roofless and vaulted and to keep them safe on the ever-changing trail. Her letter spelled out—in specific, accurate, judicious, syllabus-attending, evidence-based detail—why my teaching and role-modeling had meant so much to her. Her work had been as unfailingly brave as it was smart, and I was gladdened and touched that she'd taken the time to write to me.

> Another secret: what she said, though, handing
> me the letter.
> That.

> Generation by generation.
> That.

> Questions: if he'd made it to the mountains of the west with me, would a cougar have ended him? If he hadn't died, would I ever have gone?

In the east, we ditched the trails on the back slopes of Battell and saw things no one sees. He carried water, food for us both. A first aid kit. The means to make fire.

> A secret: there's the 'we' again—the Us, one being in two bodies. It's world-making, that kind of love. It is both key and door. The city wall. The lapis tablet.

> Question: is it a gift, when it's mortal? It destroys the world, loss like that.

We were Gilgamesh and Enkidu, except of course the closer we got to the end the more I saw our roles had reversed. It was me that was going to be left, holding his pulseless, cooling body on the floor and keening, refusing to let go. His last breath caught in the palm of my left hand, where it remains.

It was going to be me ripping my robes and finery, covering myself with ash, hacking off ropes of my hair and walking west to lose my god damned mind and hatch a plan to kill death myself: I could not allow there to be another loss like this.

> *Six days and seven nights I mourned over him*
> *and would not allow him to be buried*
> *until a maggot fell out of his nose.*

> *Panther of the wilderness, fleet wild ass of the mountain,*
> *swift mule: what is this sleep that has seized you? You*
> *have turned dark and do not hear me.*
> *His eyes did not move. I touched his heart, but it beat no longer.*

> *How I covered my friend's face like a bride, swooping*
> *down over him like an eagle. Like a lioness deprived of*
> *her cubs, I paced. Sheared off my curls, casting away*
> *finery as abomination.*
> *After you died I donned the skin of a lion and roamed the wilderness.*

> I burned my beloved brother bride
> so there would be no maggots.

Once, drawn by chorus, we came to the brink of a long, descending steep. Beavers had terraced it with mathematical precision: pool, dam, drop, pool; pool, dam, drop, pool. It went on and on, all the way down the slope, and in each pond-step, the voices of a hundred thousand oak toads.

Church, see? Creeping down the sodden steeps, listening.
Home. A league of gardens.

At the bottom, the last pond held and the way down from there became a gully punctuated by erratics from past floods.

Lining the gully: ten thousand dog-toothed violets, golden and spotty.

In Iraq, a recently discovered tablet describes Gilgamesh's forest in language we have never heard.

What likelihood is there, of finding such a stone unbroken among all our vile wreckage?

It tells of hubris, destruction of the sacred. It also tells of awe, of monkeys—monkeys! In Iraq!—and tropical vine.

It tells of the role of the forest guardian Humbaba. In fresh-discovered lines, the guardian's work is described stamen by fruit by animal by root.

It tells of humility, from the root *humus*: that rich, dark layer of soil composed of all that has gone before; death and rot from which all wisdom comes.

Once there was. Once we found. It was all torn from the ground.

Utnapishtim said: "I will reveal to you, Gilgamesh, a secret that is hidden, a secret of the gods I will tell you—"

> A statement:
> It's elegy, the missing tablet, as all nature poetry is now.
>
> A question:
> You know that, right?
>
> The question of the epic:
> How do we go on—heart open—
> in the presence of death?

Gilgamesh sat down weeping. Tears streamed over the sides of his nose.

When he returned to Uruk empty-handed, he went back to the beginning. He concerned himself with the building of foundations.

There is no map.

There is only the story.

Acknowledgments

"Pinks" appeared in *Crab Orchard Review*. "Landscape With Dead Beloved" and "Songs for the Dead Beloved" appeared in *Taos Journal of International Poetry and Art*. "Nightwalk," "This Dream is About You," and "Ghost Walk With Dead Beloved" appeared in *Life and Legends*. "Walking the Dogs Between Blizzards" and "What the Forest Said" appeared in *qaartsiluni*. "Freezing Up Blue" appeared in *Nth Position*.

Where I have quoted or paraphrased *The Epic of Gilgamesh*, I have used Maureen Kovacs' excellent translation (Stanford University Press, 1989).

Every crone-mother-maiden-witch-familiar gratitude and love to the generous and patient oracle that is Ruth Thompson, and to Don Mitchell for his patient work on a difficult book design and his beautiful cover art.

Gratitude, too, to all my generous early readers.

Sweet Nothings

Riding shotgun, Gilgamesh gives me the romantic eyes and reaches a paw in my direction. Do the shoulder-thing, he's saying. Obedient to his lowered lashes, I barely ruffle the fur on his shoulder in big, slow circles while we drive. It's one of our just-between-us habits.

His ruff is soggy from the lake, where he had to impress a girl with his mad swimming skills—a dunking I was glad of, since it took care of the eau de deadthing he had applied so urgently when he saw her coming down the trail.

Beneath the fierce iridescence of his crowlike coat, a lambswool and eider sponge. Winter underfur, blowing out. We brush whole dogs from his throat, the thick line down his knobby spine: the local birds and squirrels have the best-insulated nests in the County.

In the passenger seat, his silvered eyes close. He sways in time to my circling ruffle. Radiates perfect confidence of being loved.

It's a tangible thing, his contentment. Ripples from a tossed luckstone—only scent. Only sense.

"You know, Gabriel Garcia Marquez gave you away," I tell him later, spooning his greying warmth, his knobby spine. *"I can tell you're an angel by the way you smell of flowers."*

Gilly shrugs. Says: *"Can you bring me some candy-medicine? I overdid it at the lake today."*

Real angels are like that.

Their bones ache.

Their breath smells of peanut butter and baby-aspirin.

If I could just get this one thing right—

www.ingramcontent.com/pod-product-compliance
Lightning Source LLC
Chambersburg PA
CBHW020907080526
44589CB00011B/479